Three Contemporary Poets
of New England:
William Meredith,
Philip Booth, and
Peter Davison

Twayne's United States Authors Series

Warren French, Editor
Indiana University, Indianapolis

TUSAS 437

WILLIAM MEREDITH
Photograph by Alan Decker,
News Office, Connecticut College

PHILIP BOOTH
Photograph by Camera North

PETER DAVISON
Photograph courtesy of Peter Davison

Three Contemporary Poets of New England:
William Meredith, Philip Booth, and Peter Davison

By Guy Rotella
Northeastern University

Twayne Publishers • *Boston*

Three Contemporary Poets of New England:
William Meredith, Philip Booth, and Peter Davison

Guy Rotella

Copyright © 1983 by **G. K.** Hall & Company
All Rights Reserved
Published by Twayne Publishers
A Division of **G. K.** Hall & Company
70 Lincoln Street
Boston, Massachusetts 02111

Book Production by Marne B. Sultz

Book Design by Barbara Anderson

Printed on permanent/durable acid-free
paper and bound in the United States of
America.

Library of Congress Cataloging in Publication Data

Rotella, Guy L.
  Three contemporary poets of New England.

  (Twayne's United States authors series: TUSAS 437)
  Bibliography: p. 193
  Includes index.
  1. American poetry—20th century—History and criticism.
  2. American poetry—New England—History and criticism.
  3. Meredith, William, 1919-   —Criticism and interpretation.
  4. Booth, Philip E.—Criticism and interpretation.
  5. Davison, Peter—Criticism and interpretation. I. Title. II. Series
PS323.5.R67   1983   811'.54'09   82-15773
ISBN 0-8057-7377-0

for Mary Jane

Contents

About the Author

Guy Rotella is Associate Professor of English at Northeastern University in Boston. He studied at Siena College, Northeastern University, and Boston College, where he received his doctorate in 1976. Professor Rotella is the author of *E.E. Cummings: A Reference Guide* (G.K. Hall, 1979) and has published critical essays on Robert Penn Warren, Andrew Marvell, John Crowe Ransom, A.R. Ammons, and Robert Frost, as well as his own poems.

Preface

William Meredith, Philip Booth, and Peter Davison are diverse poets whose thematic and technical interests vary widely. The three do, however, share a relationship to the general development of contemporary American poetry from academic to experimental norms. They also share the use of New England settings and of aspects of the New England literary tradition. To an extent, these shared characteristics account for their inclusion in this study. It will be obvious, though, that these same characteristics might justify entirely different combinations of poets. A more fundamental reason for their inclusion, then, is that each has produced a substantial body of important poetry which has received far less critical attention than it deserves (thus the bibliography in this book is slender). Further, their work has particular interest and attraction for me. Of course, these remarks also indicate a rather arbitrary grouping. Moreover, the succeeding chapters quite separately survey each poet's career. Nevertheless, while the grouping of Meredith, Booth, and Davison is in part arbitrary, and while their treatments here are largely distinct, it remains true that they have much in common. The brief introduction underlines what they share, a matter only implicit elsewhere, and provides context for the individual surveys to follow, each a monograph-length treatment of one of the poets. Each survey begins with a biographical sketch and a brief general discussion of the writer's characteristic themes and techniques and of their development. It then proceeds to a book-by-book analysis of his career, paying special attention to describing and assessing those characteristic and evolving themes and techniques, and consistently offering close readings of representative poems to support the descriptions and assessments. Each chapter concludes with more specific discussion than the necessarily general introduction allows of the poet's relationship to the history of contemporary poetry in America and of his use of the New England inheritance.

My thanks to William Meredith, Philip Booth, and Peter Davison for their help with and encouragement of this project, for providing me with materials I could not otherwise have obtained, and especially for their generosity in sharing with me pre-publication materials for their most recent books. Special thanks to Francis C. Blessington and Jon Lanham, to my wife, Mary Jane, and to my editor, Warren French; each read the manuscript and made valuable suggestions for its improvement.

Guy Rotella

Northeastern University

Acknowledgments

Thanks to William Meredith for permission to quote from *Love Letter from an Impossible Land* and *Ships and Other Figures*. Grateful acknowledgment is made to Alfred A. Knopf, Inc. for permission to quote from the copyrighted works of William Meredith: *The Open Sea and Other Poems, The Wreck of the Thresher and Other Poems, Earth Walk: New and Selected Poems, Hazard, the Painter*, and *The Cheer*.

Reprinted by permission of Viking Penguin Inc.: Selections from *Letter from a Distant Land* by Philip Booth. Copyright 1951– © 1957 by Philip Booth. Selections from *The Islanders* by Philip Booth. Copyright 1952, © 1957, 1958, 1959, 1960, 1961 by Philip Booth. Selections from *Weathers and Edges* by Philip Booth. Copyright © 1959, 1961, 1962, 1963, 1964, 1965, 1966 by Philip Booth. Selections from *Margins* by Philip Booth. Copyright 1953, © 1955, 1956, 1958–70 by Philip Booth. Selections from *Available Light* by Philip Booth. Copyright © 1964, 1968, 1969, 1972, 1973, 1974, 1975, 1976 by Philip Booth. Selections from *Before Sleep* by Philip Booth. Copyright © 1976–1980 by Philip Booth.

Thanks to Yale University Press for permission to quote from *The Breaking of the Day* by Peter Davison.

Excerpts from *The City and the Island* by Peter Davison. Copyright © 1964, 1965, 1966 Peter Davison. Reprinted by permission of Atheneum Publishers. Excerpts from *Pretending to Be Asleep* by Peter Davison. Copyright © 1967, 1968, 1969, 1970 Peter Davison. Reprinted by permission of Atheneum Publishers. Excerpts from *Walking the Boundaries: Poems 1957–1974* by

Chronologies

William (Morris) Meredith

1919   Born 9 January in New York City. Father: William Morris Meredith; mother: Nelley Keyser Meredith. (Raised in Darien, Connecticut. Educated at the Lenox School, Massachusetts.)

1940   A.B., Princeton University, *magna cum laude.*

1940–1941   Copy boy, then reporter, for the *New York Times.*

1941–1942   Private, USAAC.

1942–1946   Navy pilot, lieutenant.

1944   *Love Letter from an Impossible Land,* Yale Series of Younger Poets Award.

1946–1950   Woodrow Wilson Fellow, later instructor in English and Resident Fellow in Creative Writing, Princeton University.

1948   *Ships and Other Figures.*

1950–1951   Associate Professor of English, University of Hawaii, Honolulu.

1952–1954   USNR; served as naval aviator in Korean War; promoted to lieutenant commander; awarded two Air Medals.

1955   Began continuing career as member of the English faculty, Connecticut College, New London.

1958   *The Open Sea and Other Poems.* Wrote the libretto for Peter Whiton's opera, *The Bottle Imp.*

1958–1962   Taught, summers, at the Bread Loaf School of English in Vermont.

1963–1965   Member, Connecticut Commission on the Arts.

1964   *The Wreck of the Thresher and Other Poems.* Elected Chancellor of the Academy of American Poets. Translated *Alcools: Poems 1898–1913* by Guillaume Apollinaire.

1965–1966   Resident Fellow in Creative Writing, Princeton University.

1966   Awarded the Loines prize of the National Institute of Arts and Letters.

1968   With Mackie L. Jarrell, edited and introduced *18th Century English Minor Poets.* Member, National Institute of Arts and Letters (as of 1976, American Academy and National Institute of Arts and Letters; Secretary since 1980).

1970   *Earth Walk: New and Selected Poems.*

1971   Received the Van Wyck Brooks Award.

1975   *Hazard, the Painter.*

1978   Henry B. Plant Professor of English, Connecticut College.

1978–1980   Consultant in Poetry to the Library of Congress.

1979   Bain-Swiggett Lecturer, Spring term, Princeton University. International Vaptsarov Prize for Literature, Sofia, Bulgaria.

1980   *The Cheer.*

Chronologies
Philip Booth

1925   Born 8 October in Hanover, New Hampshire. Father: Edmund H. Booth, Professor of English at Dartmouth College; mother: Jeanette Hooke Booth. (Raised in Hanover and in Castine, Maine. Educated at Vermont Academy.)

1944–1945   Aviation trainee, USAAC.

1946   Married Margaret Tillman.

1948   A.B., Dartmouth College.

1949   M.A., Columbia University.

1949–1950   Instructor in English, Bowdoin College.

1950–1951   Assistant to Director of Admissions, Dartmouth College.

1954–1961   Instructor and, later, Assistant Professor, Wellesley College.

1955   Awarded Bess Hokin Prize by *Poetry* for "Letter from a Distant Land."

1957   *Letter from a Distant Land*, 1956 Lamont Poetry Selection.

1958–1959   Guggenheim Fellow.

1961   *The Islanders.*

1961–1965   Associate Professor, Syracuse University.

1962   Phi Beta Kappa Poet, Columbia University.

1964   Guggenheim Fellow. Began continuing career as Professor of English and Poet-in-Residence, Syracuse University. Currently divides his year between teaching in the Creative Writing Program at Syracuse and living and writing at his family home in Castine, Maine.

1966   *Weathers and Edges.*

1967 Received National Institute of Arts and Letters Award.

1968 Rockefeller Foundation Fellow.

1970 *Margins: A Sequence of New and Selected Poems.* Awarded the Theodore Roethke Prize for a poem in *Poetry Northwest.*

1976 *Available Light.*

1979 Granted National Endowment for the Arts Fellowship.

1980 *Before Sleep.*

Peter Davison

1928	Born 27 June in New York City. Father: Edward Davison, Anglo-American poet; mother: Natalie Weiner Davison. (Raised in Boulder, Colorado, and elsewhere. Educated at the Fountain Valley School, Colorado Springs.)
1949	A.B., Harvard College, *magna cum laude*, Phi Beta Kappa.
1949–1950	Fulbright Scholar, St. John's College, Cambridge University.
1950–1951	First reader, Harcourt, Brace and Co.
1951–1953	Served in the United States Army, Psychological Warfare Division; rose to the rank of sergeant.
1953–1955	Assistant Editor, Harcourt, Brace and Co.
1955	Left New York City and moved to Cambridge, Massachusetts.
1955–1956	Assistant to the Editor, Harvard University Press.
1956–1959	Associate Editor, Atlantic Monthly Press.
1959	Married Jane Auchincloss Truslow.
1959–1964	Executive Editor, Atlantic Monthly Press.
1964	*The Breaking of the Day*, Yale Series of Younger Poets Award.
1964–1979	Director, Atlantic Monthly Press.
1966	*The City and the Island.*
1967–1970	Board Member, National Translation Center.
1968	Purchased Gloucester house (moved there permanently in 1979).
1968–1980	Member, Board of Directors, Atlantic Monthly Company.
1970	*Pretending to Be Asleep.*

THREE CONTEMPORARY POETS OF NEW ENGLAND

1971 *Dark Houses.*

1971–1972 Sabbatical year in Rome writing *Half Remembered* and new poems in *Walking the Boundaries.*

1972 Resumed directorship, Atlantic Monthly Press. Began continuing position as Poetry Editor of the *Atlantic Monthly.* Received National Institute of Arts and Letters / American Academy of Arts and Letters Award.

1973 *Half Remembered: A Personal History.*

1974 *Walking the Boundaries: Poems 1957–1974.*

1977 *A Voice in the Mountain.*

1978 Edited and prefaced *Hello Darkness: The Collected Poems of L.E. Sissman.* Member, the Corporation of Yaddo.

1979 Became Senior Editor, Atlantic Monthly Press, his present position.

1980 Edited and prefaced *The World of Farley Mowat.*

1981 *Barn Fever.*

Chapter One

Introduction

Contemporary Poetry

The history of contemporary American poetry (roughly, poetry since 1945, a poetry still being written and too close to us for certain definition) is the history of a dramatic shift from so-called "academic" to experimental poetry. Less dramatically, and at varying rates and in varying degrees, this shift also characterizes the particular careers of William Meredith, Philip Booth, and Peter Davison. Each begins with poems in the academic style and eventually moves toward more experimental modes. To give these terms meaning, some background is needed.

Contemporary poetry began with an orthodox style derived from and decreed by the successes of modernist poetry, and more important, the successes of the New Criticism's response to it. Because many practitioners of this now orthodox style were associated with colleges and universities (either as professors or poets-in-residence), because its intellectual modes made it appropriate for classroom study, and because it seemed rule-oriented, the style was termed "academic." The poetry it produced, and produces, is marked by regular rhyme, regular meters, and regular stanza forms; by complexity, irony, ambiguity, and paradox; by a relative impersonality of subject, voice, and tone; by literary and other forms of cultural allusiveness; by implied emphasis on the ordering power of the rational; and by a sense of the poem as an autotelic object, a self-contained, self-referential, closed system. It is often indirect, intellectual, highly condensed, and accessible only to the initiated.

Despite the developmental shift away from it asserted above, the academic style has remained viable throughout the contemporary period. Poets whose careers began after the various anti-academic experimental rebellions were well under way make significant use of its methods. And elements of those methods persist in the work of many contemporary poets, Meredith, Booth, and Davison among them. Nevertheless, the academic *orthodoxy* did begin to collapse in the middle-to-late 1950s, when more and more poets began to find the principles more constricting than liberating. These poets sought new modes and new masters, turning from the intellectual, impersonal, paradoxical, often formalistic poetries of T. S. Eliot, John Crowe Ransom, and W. H. Auden to the poetries of Walt Whitman and William Carlos Williams, with their use of more common language, setting, and subject, their tendency to frank personal expression, their relative directness, and their experiments in technique.

The revolt against academic orthodoxy thus begun was itself heterodox; that is, it was not a single rebellion, but a series of rebellions marked by a variety of aesthetic ideas and attitudes. Many of these rebellions' battles were waged by groups of poets, some of them tight coteries with elaborate manifestos, others loose associations of members with shared technical or thematic interests. The most important of these "schools" are the Beats, the Black Mountain or Projectivist poets, the confessional poets, the poets of the "deep image," and the New York poets.[1] Other battles in the anti-academic revolt were waged by poets who remained independent of movements or schools and reacted against academic formalism in more individual ways. Meredith, Booth, and Davison belong in this category. (Even in placing them there, it must be remarked once more that their own shifts from the academic to the experimental are more gradual and less dramatic than the word "revolt" implies.)

In any case, this is not the place for a history of these groups' complex, often overlapping, sometimes conflicting rebellions against the academic norm. It is the place to state the collective characteristics of the experimental poetry resulting from those rebellions, a poetry that, by the early-to-middle 1970s, had itself become a norm. The poetry promulgated and produced by the experimental poets is typically irregular in rhyme or is unrhymed. Its meters and forms are organic, that is, often irregular, arising and taking their shapes from within the particulars of the individual poet and poetic occasion and being validated by those particulars, rather than formalistic, that is, regular, arising and taking their validity from literary tradition and then being imposed on the poem from outside. Contemporary poetry in the experimental style is usually less willfully difficult and intellectual than academic poetry; often includes, encourages, and values elements of the non- and anti-rational that are usually excluded, controlled, or devalued by the rational in the academic style; and is generally more direct and accessible in its diction and meanings than are poems in that style. It is frequently autobiographical and generally personal in subject, voice, and tone. And avoidance of arcane or high-cultural allusiveness is typical, as is the replacement of the academic view of the poem as autotelic object, a self-referential, closed system, with a view of it as an open process, often fragmentary and provisional, and often engaged with the social and political world.

To return to Meredith, Booth, and Davison, and to repeat, each began as an academic poet and has moved in the direction of experimental poetry. However, none of them has yet wholly abandoned the academic mode or wholly accepted the experimental one, and probably none will. Indeed, it is precisely their balancing, unbalancing, and rebalancing of the claims and counterclaims of those modes, of the formally traditional and the organic, the rational and the non-rational, and the impersonal and the personal, and of those modes' antithetical views of the poem as closed object and open process that relates the poets to one another and places them squarely within the central concerns of contemporary poetry in the United States.

New England

Meredith, Booth, and Davison are also related by their use
of New England settings and of aspects of the New England
literary tradition. The former is simply enough explained. Literally,
if trivially, all three poets reside in New England. Booth was born
in Hanover, New Hampshire, and lives most of the year in Castine,
Maine. Meredith and Davison are transplanted New Yorkers (the
latter by way of Colorado), who now live in New London, Con-
necticut, and West Gloucester, Massachusetts, respectively. All
have spent most of their mature years—most of their writing years—
in New England, and New England landscapes (largely rural,
sometimes rural-suburban ones) play significant roles in their
work. As for their relations to the New England literary tradition,
one specific connection can be mentioned: all three were personally
and poetically influenced by Robert Frost. It would be folly to
attempt to trace here their more general relations to that tradition.
The tradition itself is complex, and each poet responds to it dif-
ferently. Nevertheless, a few remarks about three related aspects
of the New England inheritance that these poets seem most to
feel—the New England emblem tradition, literary transcendental-
ism, and what might be called post-transcendentalism—may pro-
vide some useful context.

The earliest New England writers, the Puritans, believed that
all natural and human events, however small or seemingly in-
significant, were direct indicators of spiritual truths. As a way of
knowing reality and super-reality, this belief lost force in the
rational, deistic eighteenth century. In somewhat altered form
it regained power—a power now more philosophical and aesthetic
than religious—in the nineteenth century transcendentalist con-
cept that it is through an intimate relation with unspoiled nature
that man can best come to know and express himself, this world,
and the world beyond this world. Against this view stood, and
stands, another, largely scientific one which asserts the utter in-
difference of nature to man and his concerns. The conflict en-
gendered by the confrontation of these opposing ideas and their

post-transcendentalist implications informs much of the poetry of such major New England writers as Emily Dickinson, Robert Frost, and Wallace Stevens. Their philosophical nature poetry addresses certain related questions with a sometimes hopeful, often desolate skepticism. Is the tendency to read facts as types of larger meanings a legitimate or false one? Are our ways of understanding and ordering reality acts of objective discovery or mere impositions of a willfully subjective self? What are the possibilities and limits of human knowledge and of poetry? In their own quite different and contemporary ways, Meredith, Booth, and Davison continue to explore such questions, questions broader than, but also very much part of, the New England inheritance. It is this, and the frequently local settings in which those explorations take place, that makes them recognizably New England poets.

Chapter Two

"A Dark Question Answered Yes": The Poems of William Meredith

Biographical Sketch

William Meredith was born 9 January 1919, in New York City. He grew up in Darien, Connecticut, and was educated at the Lenox School, in Massachusetts, and at Princeton University, from which he graduated *magna cum laude* in 1940. He was interested in poetry from an early age, interested, he has said, "for rather impure and escapist reasons," and has been writing poems "as much as laziness allowed" since he was about eight.[1] In the year after his graduation from Princeton, Meredith became first a copy boy and then a reporter for the *New York Times*, and, with the encouragement of poets Allen Tate and Muriel Rukeyser, began to write poetry more seriously. During World War II he served first as a private in the United States Army Air Corps, in 1941–42, and then, for the remainder of the war, as a Navy pilot, stationed first in the Aleutians and later in the Hawaiian Islands. This experience produced many of the poems that, in 1943, two friends of Meredith at Princeton, Willard Thorp and Arthur Mizener, put together in a manuscript which they submitted to the Yale Series of Younger Poets, then edited by Archibald MacLeish. The manuscript was accepted and published, with a preface by MacLeish, as *Love Letter from an Impossible Land*, in 1944, when its author was still on active duty.

After the war, Meredith returned to Princeton, where he remained from 1946 to 1950, as a Woodrow Wilson Fellow and, later, as instructor in English and Resident Fellow in Creative Writing. The latter of these positions involved his appointment as assistant to the critic R. P. Blackmur in his creative writing courses, a post in which for several years Meredith alternated with the poet John Berryman, who would later become a close friend. During this period his second book, *Ships and Other Figures* (1948), was published.

In 1950 and 1951 Meredith was associate professor of English at the University of Hawaii in Honolulu. A naval reservist, he was called to active duty in the Korean War, and served from 1952 to 1954 as a carrier pilot; he was promoted to the rank of lieutenant commander and awarded two Air Medals. Meredith has said of these years that they seemed to give him a new start as a writer.[2] In 1955 Meredith returned to university teaching at Connecticut College, in New London, where since 1964 he has held the rank of professor. In 1978 he was named Henry B. Plant Professor of English. Each summer from 1958 to 1962 he taught at the Bread Loaf School of English in Vermont. There he became acquainted with Robert Frost, whom he accompanied on a reading tour in 1960. From 1961 through 1977 he was intermittently a staff member of the Bread Loaf Writers Conference; in 1965–66, he was Resident Fellow in Creative Writing at Princeton and, in 1979, Bain-Swiggett Lecturer at Princeton.

In addition to writing and college teaching, Meredith has had a continuing interest in other arts and in public secondary education. He served from 1963 to 1965 as a member of the Connecticut Commission on the Arts and in 1969–70 was the first Writer in Residence of the International Poetry Forum in Pittsburgh. From 1955 to 1956 he was opera critic for the *Hudson Review* and later, as a Ford Foundation Fellow, studied with the New York City and Metropolitan Opera companies. At Princeton and then at Connecticut College, he was involved in various programs for black high school students, and from 1964 through 1968 he directed Connecticut College's Humanities Upward Bound Program.

Meredith's third book, *The Open Sea and Other Poems*, appeared in 1958. Subsequent books of poetry are: *The Wreck of the Thresher and Other Poems* (1964), *Earth Walk: New and Selected Poems* (1970), *Hazard, the Painter* (1975), and *The Cheer* (1980). Meredith's other publications include a selection of Shelley's poems, which he edited and introduced (1962), and a translation of Guillaume Apollinaire's *Alcools: Poems 1898–1913* (1964). He has written several essays and reviews and also authored the libretto for Peter Whiton's opera, *The Bottle Imp*, produced in Wilton, Connecticut, in 1958. (Meredith's interest in opera, by the way, was part of the basis for his long acquaintance with W. H. Auden.)

Among Meredith's honors are the Yale Series of Younger Poets Award for 1943; the Harriet Monroe Memorial Prize and the Oscar Blumenthal Prize, in 1944 and 1953 respectively (both of these for poems in *Poetry* magazine); two Rockefeller Foundation grants, for criticism in 1948, and for poetry in 1968; a grant in literature from the National Institute of Arts and Letters in 1958; a Ford Foundation Fellowship for Drama in 1960; a *Hudson Review* fellowship in 1966; the Loines Award of the National Institute of Arts and Letters, also in 1966; the Van Wyck Brooks Award in 1971; a grant from the National Endowment for the Arts in 1972; and a Guggenheim Fellowship in 1976. Meredith is a member of the National Institute of Arts and Letters and, since his election in 1964, a chancellor of the Academy of American Poets. In 1979 he traveled, as one of a delegation of eight American poets, to an international poetry festival in Struga, Yugoslavia, where he read his own poems and spoke at a symposium on the Language of Poetry in Defense of Human Speech. Also in 1979 he received the International Vaptsarov Prize for Literature in Sofia, Bulgaria. From 1978 through 1980 Meredith was Consultant in Poetry to the Library of Congress.

Theme, Technique, and Development

William Meredith's major theme involves the efforts of imagination and intellect to order the chaos of the self and of the world, to overcome the resistance of life and experience to significance and form. He writes, in the phrase of Wallace Stevens, a poetry "of the mind in the act of finding / What will suffice." He seeks an art and life of meaning and value. The goal of this search does not alter appreciably as Meredith's work develops. What does alter is the degree of confidence he feels in any of the search's many methods and results, and his identification and understanding of what and where the threats to its successful completion and to the maintenance of its gains are located. This development includes recognition that the very urge to order itself may be among those threats. This can be put another way. In a recent Library of Congress lecture Meredith defined poetry as "accurate praise." The modifier is crucial. What he has always sought is affirmation, but what he has come more and more to see is that praise—to be accurate, to be true—must include what resists as well as what releases it.

In terms of technique, Meredith began his career writing in the academic manner. Many of the poems in his first two books are imitative of poetry in the metaphysical mode the academic poets favored. However, even in these early collections there are indications of the slow, relatively undramatic shifting that begins in earnest in his third volume and continues in his recent work, a shifting toward a poetry more personal in content and voice, more colloquial in diction, more straightforward—and, paradoxically, more complex—in feeling and statement, more open and organic in form, more provisional, more suspicious of the claims of the rational, and more willing to consider the claims of the non-rational. Clearly, then, although Meredith is often categorized as an unreconstructed academic, his technical development places him within the typical progression of contemporary verse. It will become clear that, at the same time and for all his technical evolution, his more or less continuous thematic commitment to accurate, affirming resistance to the chaos of self and world rather than immersed acceptance of it places him directly in the line of the academic poets and their modern ancestors.

Love Letter from an Impossible Land

Love Letter from an Impossible Land (1944) was published when William Meredith was twenty-five. A few of its poems were composed while he was still an undergraduate. Not surprisingly, much of the book is imitative, written, as Meredith himself would later say, in a "borrowed rhetoric."[3] In spite of this, *Love Letter from an Impossible Land* indicates what will become Meredith's continuing and developing themes and techniques.

When the book appeared, a volume in Yale University's prestigious series for younger poets, it was introduced by the poet Archibald MacLeish, dedicated to Princeton professor Christian Gauss and his wife, and bore on its title page the military rank of its author. As Richard Howard has pointed out, this extraordinary series of institutional signs is reflected in the institutional forms of the poems:[4] many sonnets and near sonnets, "strict songs," quatrains, even variations of the highly artificial French rondeau. These rigorous forms give the volume the appearance of consistency; however, that appearance is somewhat illusory. Even the commitment to traditional forms is less complete than it seems. In fact, it is possible to break the poems of *Love Letter from an Impossible Land* almost cleanly into two groups.

The poems of the first group (mostly early ones) are those marked by the self-conscious literary imitation noted above. The literature they imitate is very much that sanctioned by the academic establishment. Echoes of George Herbert, Allen Tate, Auden, the later Yeats, and other seventeenth- and twentieth-century metaphysical poets are everywhere in them (although there are interesting exceptions, hints of Arnold and Tennyson, for instance). At any rate, here is Meredith straining after Yeats (while imitating Herbert): "Only an outward-aching soul / Can hold in high disdain these ties" ("Airman's Virtue"). Impressive, no doubt, but in someone else's voice. Here is Meredith in an Auden mode:

> Sir, today is vouched for, and what is owing
> Will be paid, all that long borrowing;
> Let the day's portents and its tedious sad history
> Prompt the guarantors to no defection.[5]

The sonnet-like poem ends with these lines: "Doubting as children, they were healed at a terrible spa, / And now are eager to speak for the least stammerer," echoing Auden's own sonnet-like "Petition." Beyond such specific imitations, and there are more of them, the poems of this type are also often marked by more general and equally self-conscious adherence to other characteristics of what was becoming the academic style: allusiveness, impersonality, and intellectual contortion.

The allusiveness is self-evident. Impersonality in these poems takes the form not so much of invented, identifiable personae (such as, for instance, the speaker of T. S. Eliot's "The Love Song of J. Alfred Prufrock") as of a disembodied, unlocatable voice. Listen to the distance and indirection of the speaker of this poem:

> Who comes upon one standing in a door,
>   That with a sigh tries different sorrows on,
>   Thinking how best to speed a lover gone,
> Whether this leave or that becomes her more,
> Knowing him there beside her all the while;
>   Or who hears lovers worry of the dawn
>   Before the white of evening quite has worn
> And they not knowing dawn, and sees them smile;
> Let him not presume what thing it was
>   He saw enacted in a smile or sigh

Till he pass and the door be shut and the day be high
And the lover wonders how his lover does.
With such confused denouement the play ends
That none but the spectator comprehends.

(13)

Intellectual difficulty, or, rather, the appearance of it, in this volume is more often the result of syntactical contortion than of real complexity. Note, for instance, how a fairly accessible statement about desire and remorse is made momentarily puzzling by its twisted, condensed construction:

Do not say to the gay game nay now lover
Under cover of love enough; does puritan twinge
Predict, against respite from passion, real change?
No, we shall want again later and greatly all over.

(19)

But it is pointless to criticize the apprentice work of a young poet imitating the received masters of his time as he learns his craft. In their proper context these poems are impressive for the skills they frequently display and, even more so, for the developments in formal, technical, and syntactical expertise they promise. They are failures not of the academic mode itself but of their own rather artificial and forced handling of its methods.

However, *Love Letter from an Impossible Land* also contains poems of a second type, poems more personal in voice, more colloquial in language, more straightforward in feeling, and somewhat more open in form. The orders they achieve are often convincingly earned against real threats. The last point is essential. Poems of both types are concerned with intellectual and imaginative acts of ordering; indeed, almost all of Meredith's poems are so concerned. However, while those acts in the earlier poems of *Love Letter from an Impossible Land* are often programmed, predictable, even smug (note, for instance, the tendency to the imperative mode), in the later poems they are often dramatic, surprising, and moving. The key to these changes seems to be Meredith's war experience. He has indirectly suggested this himself: "During the War, . . . I found myself relying on my writing to make sense of an experience and a world for which nothing in a protected and rather unobservant childhood had prepared me."[6] It may be unfair to Meredith's candor, but it is difficult not to see the earlier poems of *Love Letter from an Impossible Land* as issuing from protected unobservance and the later ones as gaining power from the war's challenge to what seems to have been a comfortably habitual orderliness. Perhaps Meredith needed an impossible land to challenge such habits.

Before we look at these more successful poems, however, a word about the general nature of Meredith's war poems. Although among the best to have emerged from World War II and clearly alert to war's horrors of waste and destruction, they are basically poems of duty, accepting the necessity and legitimacy of the war that is their context. As Meredith has said, "World War II was very much more plausible than any violence that the nation has been involved with since."[7] Aptly described by Richard Howard as constituting "a lamentable genre but a real distinction," Meredith's war poems are not protest poems. Rather, they are poems that record, complain of, and then struggle to comprehend and accept the complexities of human nature, the facts of life and death.

One of the best in *Love Letter from an Impossible Land* is "Notes for an Elegy," where the very title indicates a sense of the provisional, a lack of assurance about the efficacy of restorative institutions in the face of destruction and death. This perception is far from the comfortable stances of the earlier poems. In irregular meter and unrhymed stanzas "Notes for an Elegy" questions the comforting claims of pastoral elegy as it describes the death of an airman, wrecked on a training flight. With the shared fatalism of a committed fellow pilot, the speaker insists on the necessary calculus of such a death ("in practice the martyrdom has been quiet, statistical, / A fair price. This is what airmen believe"). At the same time, though, and in the same direct, factual language, he expresses a feeling that moots such mathematics:

> Note that he had not fought one public battle,
> Met any fascist with his skill, but died
> As it were in bed, the waste conspicuous;
> This is a costly wreck and costly to happen on.
>
> (36)

With faith and feeling present and not opposed, the poem proceeds to a richly inconclusive conclusion, one filled with duty and desperation: "The morning came up foolish with pink clouds / To say that God counts ours a cunning time, / Our losses part of an old secret, somehow no loss." Thus, we are left with neither easy comfort nor easy cynicism. Is the "cunning" that of skillful knowledge or knowing deceit? Does God count "our losses" "no loss" because they are a meaningless irrelevance or because they have a real, if mysteriously secret, value? In this more personal, more organic poem, with its more natural and colloquial expression and its replacement of literary allusiveness with reference to a local time and place, the possibilities are left open. In it, there is a skeptical hope for order and affirmation that fully recognizes the threats of chaos and despair.

The volume's title poem also demonstrates gains in force, feeling, and depth of conviction stemming from the war poems' shifts in modes of expression. In epistolary direct address and an easily moving blank verse "Love Letter from an Impossible Land" describes the islands where Meredith is stationed:

> All the charts and history you can muster
> Will not make them real as fog is real
> Or crystal as a certain hour is clear
> If you can wait.
>   Write to me often, darling.
>
> (38)

In the way that final, subjectively imperative request, triggered by the idea of waiting, interrupts the objective description there is a strenuous expression of loneliness and desire. Similarly, these lines break into a catalog of pictorial detail: "Now I am convinced there is nothing to fear, / Now on these islands you are all I want." As do these, from near the poem's end: "We lie in khaki rows, no two alike, / Needing to be called by name / And saying women's names." The entire piece creates an impressive balancing of the contrasting emotions generated by war's dangers, duty's demands, and love's needs, by the conflicting claims of the tempting beauties of the alien landscape and the familiar and unaltering attractions of home.

Another of this first book's fine later poems, "June: Dutch Harbor," is also set in the Aleutians of Meredith's war experience. Like "Notes for an Elegy" and "Love Letter from an Impossible Land," it is unrhymed, colloquial, metrically and stanzaically irregular, and personal in subject and voice. Like the latter, it begins with an active and detailed description that defines place:

> In June, which is still June here, but once removed
> From other Junes, chill beardless high-voiced cousin season,
> The turf slides grow to an emerald green.
> There between the white-and-black of the snow and ash,
> Between the weak blue of the rare sky
> Or the milkwhite languid gestures of the fog,
> And the all-the-time wicked terminal sea.
>
> (41)

The island chain is a magical kingdom where the lush flowers have little regard for "precedent" ("Violets the size of pansies"). Yet if the whole chain is a bird sanctuary, it is also a military reservation where the flying is, ironically, not safe but dangerous ("above the always-griping sea / That bitches at the bitter rock the mountains throw to it"), and done only "with the permission— subject always to revoke— / Of the proper authorities," naval and otherwise. Were it not for such facts, the life of the pilots in this miraculous land might make a beautiful, heroic myth; however, the facts will not be stilled. In lines that might be as much about poetry as flying, and that tersely suggest what separates these war poems from the earlier weak and artificial imitations, Meredith expresses a sense of order at once profoundly threatened and precariously possessed: "Even without flaps there is a safe minimum; / Below that the bottom is likely to drop out." From this colloquial recognition the poem proceeds to an ambiguous statement of affirmation and doubt: "Some of the soldiers pressed flowers in June, indicating faith, / The one who knew all about birds spun in that month. / It is hard to keep your mind on war, with all that green." Is faith rewarded or mocked, real or illusion? Did the one who knew about birds spin a mythic tale of optimistic augury or did his plane spin out and crash when his attention lapsed or shifted? Is the cyclical green of spring in even so bleak a land a sign of hope against the momentary fact of war, or a trick that distracts us from the proper concerns of the moment or from the memory of those who died in a noble cause? The answer to all these is something like a yes, a yes that adumbrates the complexities of the speaker's deeply thought and felt position.

The best poems in *Love Letter from an Impossible Land* are, then, stylistically quite different from the less effective earlier ones: more personal in subject and voice, more organic in meter and form, and more colloquial in diction and syntax. At the same time, though, their less complex forms embody a more complex, and so more convincing, intellectual and emotional commemoration. Indeed, their surface accessibility is the very sign of their depth. Thus, it would be an oversimplification to see all the gains of the later poems as coming from an abandonment of the earlier ones' formal and impersonal proclivities. In fact, many war poems, like the sonnet "In Memoriam Stratton Christensen," successfully retain traditional forms and impersonal voices:

> Laughing young man and fiercest against sham,
>   Then you have stayed at sea, at feckless sea,
>   With a single angry curiosity
> Savoring fear and faith and speckled foam?
> A salt end to what was sweet begun:
>   Twenty-three years and your integrity
>   And already a certain number touched like me
> With a humor and a hardness from the sun.
>
> Without laughter we have spent your wit
>   In an unwitnessed fight at sea, perhaps not won,
>   And whether wisely we shall never know;
> But like Milton's friend's, to them that hear of it,
>   Your death is a puzzler that will tease them on
> Reckless out on the thin, important floe.
>   (45)

Hear, for example, how "Reckless" in the last line echoes the
sounds of "feckless" and "speckled" in lines two and four, as
Henry Taylor has pointed out,[8] and note how its reckless-wreckless
pun picks up and extends the complexities of tone elsewhere in
it, creating at once a complaint and a memorializing justification—
as the reference to Milton's "Lycidas" suggests, although the com-
fort here is far less institutional and sure. Whether the officer's
death has meaning and, if so, of what sort, remains mysterious
(he was lost "In an unwitnessed fight at sea, perhaps not won, /
And whether wisely we shall never know"). Yet that very mystery,
at root, the question of meaning itself, is what keeps his death
"important," what keeps.

Clearly, the gains in skill and power displayed by Meredith's
war poems derive as much from his mastering the traditions which
had earlier mastered him as from his rejection of the academic
style. What really strengthens these poems is their newfound in-
clusiveness in technique as well as content (note, for instance, the
combination of the sonnet form with colloquial and openly emo-
tional diction in "Ten-Day Leave"). This inclusiveness is born
of the presence of, and the poet's response to, real threats to

customary models of meaning and order. Even so, it is tempting to see the at least partial shift in modes from the earlier to the later poems of *Love Letter from an Impossible Land* as an early example of the shifts from academic to experimental poetry characteristic of contemporary verse. In fact, one reviewer has suggested that Meredith wrote in the 1940s the way most poets would in the 1970s.[9] Such hyperbole aside, had Meredith's next book continued in the direction indicated by some of the war poems, the temptation to endorse the hypothesis might be irresistible. However, this is not the case.

Ships and Other Figures

Ships and Other Figures was published for the Princeton University Library by the Princeton University Press in 1948. By and large, its poems retreat from the freedoms gained by the war poems' openings of self, language, and form, and by their attractive weakening of self-satisfied confidence in the powers of order and good. The poems of *Ships and Other Figures* are generally more like the worst than the best poems of *Love Letter from an Impossible Land*. In spite of the "assorted Audenries" Dudley Fitts has pointed out,[10] they are somewhat less obviously imitative than previous ones. However, to an even greater degree than the earlier volume, this one is marked by studied scholarship and the use of elaborate forms and types: sonnets, quatrains, dedicatory poems, a gift poem, a wedding poem, an *ubi sunt*, an envoi, even a heroic simile. As such a list suggests, most of the poems imply confident belief in the powers of tradition, language, imagination, and mind to order and affirm the self and the world. Unfortunately, though, the poems too rarely test or demonstrate the beliefs they depend on or the claims they make. Thus, they are often merely assertive, glib, and smugly predictable, despite certain undeniable skills and intelligence. The too-assured tone is underlined by four pages of often unnecessary and condescending explanatory notes.[11] Even the many poems based in war experience which are carried over to this postwar book usually lack the forceful truths of the earlier war poems. In fact, it is difficult to resist the thought that, at this stage, Meredith requires the fairly immediate presence of evil, of violence, of some real threat if his powerful ordering consciousness is not to level all to a dull and mild neatness.

For example, the balanced octaves of "Middle Flight," with their implied inversion of Milton's grander intentions ("Heavenly Muse . . . I thence / Invoke thy aid to my adventurous song / That with no middle flight intends to soar," *Paradise Lost*, I, ll. 6, 13–14), state and then all too easily escape a threat to the self:

> The loneliest place I know of nowadays
> Is a cumulo-nimbus cloud I seem to find
> As often as I fly; I went there first
> When the sky and a war were new, but memories now
> Are as heavy in its belly as a squall.
> It is a tall cloud, something gathered at the tops
> But opening to imprecision, at the base to rain,
> And the hope that it held five years ago is spilt.
>
> But what I mean to say about the cloud
> And its forlorn vicinity where gather
> Vapors of doubt that not our lonely day
> Shall see precipitate, is that even here
> Nobody goes alone who knows so much
> As one human love; so much I know,
> Whence hope, if any, in the covered sky,
> Choir in this uncompanionable air.
>
> (10)

The threat seems present here only to provide occasion for the affirming assertion of the saving power of human love and hope (and assertion is all it is; there is no working out, no demonstration or dramatization). This weakness is most revealed by the first, fourth, and fifth lines of the second stanza—"But what I mean to say about the cloud . . . is that even here / Nobody goes alone." The comfort offered is not in question here. What is, to repeat, is the impression created that pain was invoked solely to allow the offering of such comfort, a preconceived one at that. If this is unfair to the experiencing man behind the poem, it is not unfair to the poem. Even the penultimate line's qualifying "hope, if any," seems more compulsory than menacing. And the tendency of the poem's entire movement to recall Matthew Arnold's "Dover Beach" serves only to expose by contrast its own relative artificiality. Related flaws make many poems in *Ships and Other Figures* unconvincing. Several other poems, however, are quite successful. The descriptions of Navy ships are often powerful. "Carrier," for instance, moves at the majestic pace of the craft it describes, creating a personification which conveys the carrier pilot's care for the caring mother ship. The precise languages of fact and strategy preserve it from false feeling. The sonnet concludes:

> The planes rise heavy from her whining deck.
> Then the bomb's luck, the gun's poise and chattering,
>   The far-off dying, are her near affair;
> With her sprung creatures become weak or strong
>   She watches them down the sky and disappear,
> Heart gone, sea-bound, committed all to air.
>
> (2)

Another success, "Homeric Simile," makes convincing contemporary use of the unusually elaborate and extended comparison its title defines as it argues the merits of form in bringing even the most complex experiences to moments of miraculous clarity. The terms of the comparison are, of all things, a bombing raid and a string quartet, each with its moments of certainty, confusion, further certainty, confusion more disturbing still, and so on to eventual resolution. The raid is detailed at length. Troubled by cloud cover but confident of the mental and mechanical assurances of reckoning, the crew of a "heavy bomber" flies an unknown track. Their certainties of navigation are qualified by larger doubts about nations and war, about friends and foes. Then, suddenly, the clouds break; the crew finds itself sure again, in proper formation

and over the target. Out of this mix of feeling and the chaos of
enemy searchlights and flak comes a "penetration of the overcast":
a moment when the jewelled pattern of the target town, the
"lazy tracers," the certainties and doubts, the dropped bombs, even
dying friends—all the complex, conflicting details of the scene—
come clear and whole; they contain confusion yet are somehow
unconfused. The poem then shifts to the simile's other, briefer
term:

> Not otherwise the closing notes disclose,
> As the calm, intelligent strings do their duty,
> The hard objective of a quartet, reached
> After uncertain passage, through form observed,
> And at a risk no particle diminished.
>
> (19)

Like the crew on the bombing run, the quartet achieves its final
clarification by accepting both dangerous uncertainty and certain
form. Both clarifications contain rather than evade or ignore all
that resists them. Made convincing by its detailed use of precise,
dramatic language, this whole strange, metaphysical enterprise,
comparing war and music, becomes an example of what it de-
scribes, of the enigmatic, inclusive ordering of the apparently
antithetical.

Another convincing poem in *Ships and Other Figures* is "Do
Not Embrace Your Mind's New Negro Friend," a still pertinent
critique of too-comfortable liberalism, and a similar conflation
of the personal and political informs the otherwise very different
"A Figure from Politics." Its wry wit is a minor delight:

> The gigantic sweet conspiracy of lovers
> Who had once thought to take over everything
> Will now, I am convinced, come to nothing:
> Right about race and Russia, we were wrong
> When it came to local affairs touching each other.
>
> (5)

The slightly acrid, self-deprecating humor that fuels this poem is one of the positive developments of the volume. It suggests one way in which a tendency to too-easy orders and affirmations might be resisted and even made dramatic. Although not so successfully as in "A Figure from Politics," this device also appears in "Envoi," "Dedicatory Poem," "Blues," and "Two Figures from the Movies."

The most obvious and important development of *Ships and Other Figures* is a related, although in some ways slight and incomplete one. Several poems indicate an awakening sense of the dangers of too much order, too much reason, too easy affirmation. "Homeric Simile," for instance, returns to the complex containments of poems like "Notes for an Elegy," "Love Letter from an Impossible Land," and "June: Dutch Harbor." In comparing the relatively exotic military dangers of a bombing raid with the relatively domestic risks of the string quartet, it begins to point toward the realization that there are powerful threats to order even in the ordinary. A similar sense of the ordinary's resistance to form appears in "Dedicatory Poem." In both poems the speaker is confident that clarity can be disclosed "through form observed. / And at a risk no particle diminished." However, it is not too long a step from there to the realization that such confidence can itself become a danger. Oddly enough, the clearest indication of this new direction in Meredith's work appears in the Chaucerian "Envoi" that opens the book:

> Go, little book. If anybody asks
> Why I add poems to a time like this,
> Tell how the comeliness I can't take in
> Of ships and other figures of content
> Compels me still until I give them names;
> And how I give them names impatiently,
> As who should pull up roses by the roots
> That keep him turning on his empty bed,
> The smell intolerable and thick with loss.
>
> (1)

These last images powerfully figure forth the orderly poet's destructive tendency to violently force the world, to falsify it in order to make it fit his own desired pattern. Taken alone, such examples exaggerate the intensity of the glimmer of recognition in *Ships and Other Figures* that the drive to order itself might become a threat to sense. There are never more than indications here. And however much what they point to will eventually focus his art, this second volume is largely a backward step in Meredith's progress as a poet. The next is his breakthrough book.

The Open Sea and Other Poems

Love Letter from an Impossible Land and *Ships and Other Figures* appeared within four years; it was to be ten years before Alfred A. Knopf published Meredith's third collection in 1958. Like its predecessors, *The Open Sea and Other Poems* has pieces that are badly flawed. The ambiguities of the dedicatory poem to Donald Stauffer ("indiscriminate delight," "he could write / Commonplace books") might easily tumble into insult. The attack on Ginsberg and the Beats in "To a Western Bard Still a Whoop and a Holler Away from English Poetry" has its points but is narrow and more than a little self-congratulatory. "The Alchemist" pays tribute to Robert Frost, but suffers from sentimentality ("Laughter and tears / Can set a man apart"). "The Rainy Season," along with a few other poems, has the sound of meditative seriousness, but descends to something like cuteness:

> Like the reproof of that singular good man,
> Unknown to you, to whom you are unknown,
> Told at some length by strangers while you nod;
> And not unlike the signs in rainy bars
> That read themselves at the poor edge of sleep:
> The lie too complicated to refute:
> If you're so damn smart, why aren't you rich?
>
> (28)

Such failures, however, are relatively rare in this volume, and most of them result from the same efforts at conversational directness and complex inclusiveness that produce its finest poems. As Meredith's "breakthrough volume," *The Open Sea* breaks through on three related fronts. The first is formal. Meredith continues to enact the rage for order by which he is so often both inspired and ensnared. He extends and intensifies the formal proclivities of his earlier books, opening this one with, in sequence, a villanelle, a poem employing aspects of both villanelle and *terza rima*, a sonnet, and a sestina. And there are sonnets, quatrains, and many other, less traditional patterns throughout. However, while in the earlier books the most formal poems were often the most self-congratulatory, contrived, and unconvincing, formal control in *The Open Sea* is wedded to formal experiment and to a more openly meditative voice which speaks with a conversational, even colloquial, ease to produce natural and compelling art. With the less successful earlier poems in mind, look at "Sonnet on Rare Animals":

> Like deer *rat-tat* before we reach the clearing
> I frighten what I brought you out to see,
> Telling you who are tired by now of hearing
> How there are five, how they take no fright of me.
> I tried to point out fins inside the reef
> Where the coral reef had turned the water dark;
> The bathers kept the beach in half-belief
> But would not swim and could not see the shark.
> I have alarmed on your behalf and others'
> Sauntering things galore.
> It is this way with verse and animals
> And love, that when you point you lose them all.
> Startled or on a signal, what is rare
> Is off before you have it anywhere.

> (3)

Although one might do better to take the poem's advice and constrain the compulsion to point, note how the sonnet's three quatrains and couplet echo in their own openings and closings the drama of possession and escape that their words describe. Related points might be made about the tensions created in the poem by its delicate hovering between Elizabethan and Italian sonnet forms, by its alternation of nearly enjambed and end-stopped lines, and by its metrical variations.

Poem after poem in this volume demonstrates an achieved grace far from the often clotted clumsiness of earlier formal efforts. Here are the opening lines of *The Open Sea*'s title poem:

> We say the sea is lonely; better say
> Ourselves are lonesome creatures whom the sea
> Gives neither yes nor no for company.
>
> (2)

Such examples could easily be multiplied.

In addition to the gains in conversational ease in the formal poems of *The Open Sea*, there is a parallel gain in accessibility that removes these poems from the metaphysical contrivances of Meredith's earliest work. And it is not an accessibility purchased with the surrender of complexity. In fact, at their best these poems replace what was often merely syntactical intricacy with real knots of thought and feeling, and present them with brilliant clarity. Consider "The Illiterate," a Petrarchan sonnet using repeated end words in place of rhyme, yet employing its virtuosity in the service of mysterious clearness:

> Touching your goodness, I am like a man
> Who turns a letter over in his hand
> And you might think this was because the hand
> Was unfamiliar but, truth is, the man
> Has never had a letter from anyone;
> And now he is both afraid of what it means
> And ashamed because he has no other means
> To find out what it says than to ask someone.

His uncle could have left the farm to him,
Or his parents died before he sent them word,
Or the dark girl changed and want him for beloved.
Afraid and letter-proud, he keeps it with him.
What would you call his feeling for the words
That keep him rich and orphaned and beloved?

(10)

Once it is noted that the entire narrative of potential knowing, losing, and having is a simile for the speaker's astonishment before the qualities of a friend, relation, or lover, its details fall into place with natural, if complicated, ease. Again, examples could be multiplied but further quotation and discussion from other angles will give sufficient evidence.

A second breakthrough in *The Open Sea* is thematic. In the earlier volumes the existence and efficacy of meaning, value, and order were often simply assumed; their presence was often glibly evoked. Here, however, these existences and efficacies are less certain; the human need to constantly discover, invent, and establish order against all that threatens to dissolve it becomes a more dramatic theme, in Richard Howard's descriptive phrase, "an ethical force," especially in the book's many poems about art and art objects: architecture, painting, sculpture, music, *kabuki* theater, even topiary gardening. A single example will do. The splendidly realized sestina "Notre Dame de Chartres" is based on the story of the building of the present great basilica after the destruction by fire of the original church in the late twelfth century. The first structure had housed a tunic supposedly worn by the Virgin at the birth of Christ, one of the major relics of medieval Christianity. When the church, and the town around it, burned to the ground, the *sancta camisa*, the "blessed shirt," was not consumed. These "miracles" were taken, respectively, as signs of dissatisfaction and continuing grace. In response, Notre Dame de Chartres was built to more fittingly enshrine the sacred tunic, which "spoke to the stone that slept in the groin of France," as the poem puts it in a fine image of spiritual and architectural engendering.

Such a tale may seem a curious way to talk about man's continuing need for meaning and order; its construal of miracle is apt to strike our largely secular time as naive, as, more than a little ruefully, the poem acknowledges. At the same time, though, it insists that if our ways of understanding destruction and salvation and of paying appeasement and thanks have changed, our impulses have not: "This is our miracle: the faith that burned / Bright and erroneous, and built that house." The word "erroneous" should be stressed. The realization that all systems for wrestling shape from chaos are threatened by being necessarily relative and wrong is the sign of what renders the searchings for order and affirmation in *The Open Sea*—whether they succeed or fail— tentative, doubtful, and courageous.

"Notre Dame de Chartres," like many other poems in *The Open Sea*, admires, describes, and is committed to the creation and affirmation of artistic order, but also recognizes and includes much that resists it. This leads to consideration of the third breakthrough of *The Open Sea*, one which extends the hints in *Ships and Other Figures* of a recognition of the dangers of too much order, reason, and mild-mannered good sense. Meredith's statement that in World War II he found himself depending on his writing "to make sense of an experience and world" for which he was unprepared, and his parallel remark that it was his "two years as a carrier pilot during the Korean war that seemed to give . . . [him] another start as a writer," to initiate the discoveries of his own voice and insights recorded in *The Open Sea*, have already been quoted. Moreover, it was earlier suggested that Meredith's powerful ordering consciousness seems to require the resisting presence of real threat to prevent it from a leveling dullness. But if one is not to recommend lifelong warfare as a necessary condition for poetry, it seems fair to say that Meredith would have to begin to locate threats to the rationally controlled in a more ordinary, domestic world, and in himself. Of course, this is a critical rather than biographical formulation. At any rate, throughout *The Open Sea* (which, by the way, with the only partial exception of "Battle Problem," has no war poems) precisely such acts of location occur.

In the iambic trimeter and *ababcdcd* (and so on) rhyme scheme of Yeats's "The Fisherman," Meredith's "The Chinese Banyan" tells the story of a calm man's heart attack and explores the extremes of power and pain in even the most ordinary things:

> There is no end to the
> Deception of quiet things
> And of quiet, everyday
> People.
>
> (26)

And later: "I speak of the unremarked / Forces that split the heart." It ends with application of this domestic lesson to speaker and reader:

> this dark capacity
> Of quiet looses a fear
> That runs by analogy
> On your page, in your house, for your dear.
>
> (27)

Personal fear of death appears in several poems, the deaths of loved ones in others. "Bachelor" humorously depicts the desperations bubbling beneath the most quotidian exteriors. However, the most impressive discovery of resistances to order close to home in *The Open Sea* is, paradoxically enough, in a poem titled "An Account of a Visit to Hawaii." In a nearly allegorical discussion of landscape, history, and climate Meredith demonstrates the forces of destruction and loss that underlie even the paradisal surfaces of a tropical but not too tropical island. He thereby turns to account the very mildness that often weakened his work, converting it to the kind of threat his ordering acts require to give them weight. This is the crucial passage:

> Mildness can enervate as well as heat.
> The soul must labor to reach paradise.
> Many are here detained in partial grace
> Or partial penalty, for want of force.
>
> (19)

Such precise locations of purgatorial dangers within the self and a domesticated world serve Meredith well in the poems of *The Open Sea* and in his later volumes. Related to Meredith's discovery of resistances to reason within the ordinary is a new willingness to entertain the claims of the non-rational. This development is far from complete in *The Open Sea*, but two poems begin to indicate the shapes it will take. "On Falling Asleep by Firelight" occurs at the edge of consciousness. As the epigraph from Isaiah indicates, the poem describes a dream of the earthly paradise, a visionary Eden where the threatening alienness of beasts and of other men is replaced by a natural kindness, kinship, and sympathy that erases evil, otherness, and guilt. The poem insists that only by putting aside our experienced rational awareness of "ravening" and "guile" can we imagine such desirable perfection. At the same time, however, it also insists on the limitations of dreams. They strike us "dumb": speechless and, perhaps, stupid as well. They are only dreams ("We *dream* there is no ravening or guile," my italics). This qualified attention to the non-rational is condensed in the poem's last lines: "the heat / Turns softly on the hearth into that dust / Isaiah said would be the serpent's meat." Is this apparent interpenetration of the real fire and the vision a sign that the dream is coming true? Or is the dust of idle dreams what feeds the snake of evil, and the coming cold what wakes us again to fact? The poem is in delicate balance, but it does not, as Meredith's earlier poems would have done, wholly undercut the dream with reason. In fact, it even implies that reason itself is not enough and that the perfectly ordered world that reason (and, intriguingly here, imagination too) desires, even demands, is itself a visionary dream.

The claims of the non-rational are entertained in a very different way in another poem in *The Open Sea*, "A View of the Brooklyn Bridge." Writing about this poem in William Heyen's *American Poets in 1976*, Meredith describes it as a revelation which imprinted itself upon him: "I think all the poems I had written before this were primarily rational attempts to word accurately something I thought I understood. This poem . . . [and, he adds, to a lesser extent the earlier "Love Letter from an Impossible Land"] were irrational acts of surrender to an experience I knew very little about but which I had a sudden sense was being offered to me."[12] This is a precise description of the technical and thematic territories Meredith's poetry has so far contained and of those it now reaches out to include. Most of the poems before *The Open Sea*, and many in it, attempt to word accurately something fully grasped in rational form, formal language, and an impersonal voice. This commitment to reason and order persists. However, a very few earlier poems, a few more in *The Open Sea*, and still more in later volumes, move toward more open forms, more conversational and colloquial language, and more personal voices. They give increased attention to the less than wholly grasped, to the nonrational, the disorderly, the provisional and mysterious. Of these, "A View of the Brooklyn Bridge" is an example.

So far in discussing *The Open Sea* rather abstract categories have been used to examine Meredith's growth in it. This method is useful but also somewhat falsifying, for many poems in *The Open Sea* embody concurrently several of the developments separately discussed. Because of this, because *The Open Sea* is crucial as the volume in which Meredith discovers his characteristic voice, and because so many of its poems are so good, let us turn from categorizing and cataloging to glance at a few more of its best poems.

As noted above, several poems in *The Open Sea* explore the orderings of art. One of these, "Rus in Urbe" (the country in the city), describes a fourth-floor urban garden (containing an espaliered pear tree and a topiary yew) in order to consider the opposed claims of naturalness and artifice. The result is balance: art is lovely but often elitist and useless; for some it is what saves. The equilibrium is perfectly supported by the poem's irregular and subtly assertive placing of rhymes and by its skillful iambic variations. The related "A Korean Woman Seated by a Wall" is a more subtle consideration of the powers and limits of art to shape and redeem. Observing the woman of the title, the speaker invents a lovely and convincing tale to explain the suffering on the "alien and untranslatable" mask of her face. However, under the pressure of her actual presence his story and its assumptions and presumptions are shattered. Again, art's power to clarify life is asserted and qualified to produce rich truth.

Others of *The Open Sea*'s best poems are united by imagery and metaphor rather than theme. Several continue to tap two of Meredith's richest sources of these, the sea and trees,[13] the former most impressively in the title poem. "The Open Sea" is a many-toned assertion of the sea's blank indifference, the reality behind our sayings, fancies, and poems about it: "The sea gives neither yes nor no for company." The speaker's response comes in the final stanza, its "not yet" and "nor yet" marking his combined resistance and recognition: "Although not yet a man given to prayer, I pray / For each creature lost since the start at sea, / And give thanks that it was not I, nor yet one close to me."

Trees play a larger role in this book. In addition to pertinent poems already discussed, three more are especially fine. "The Deciduous Trees" presents an analogy of trees and men, of the stressed and tensioned forms they make to resist and outlast their bitter season. "A Botanical Trope," like "On Falling Asleep by Firelight," inverts the tendency of several poems here to expose the sentimentality of human impositions of subjective form and meaning on the world, emphasizing instead metaphor's real because properly qualified truth. Perhaps the best "tree poem" in *The Open Sea*, though, and one of the best poems in the book, is Meredith's inverted anti-pastoral elegy for his mother, "In Memoriam N.K.M. (1889–1947)." The sonnet does not complain that nature fails to reflect her death. Rather, it mourns that she did not, could not, in her dying, reflect the glory of sunset or the autumnal brightness of the trees, perhaps because her going is more "final" than such departures. The poem deserves quotation in full:

As the day takes color twice, so youth and age
Should glow remarkably. Or, like a maple's
I wish her fall had been (whose quaint April
Is still in blossom on the album's pages)
Splendid and red, which was a sere, gray loss.
Like a round maple, if that could just have been,
Whose virtuous green summer went unseen
In a mild chemistry, but at first frost
Who stuck across herself and her slight hill
Patterns no elm would dream of, crooked and true
Like the serene old trees on a chinese scroll:
This is a thing I have seen maples do.
The sun and trees glowed fiercely at the season
When she wandered listless forth bereft of reason.

(31)

The many poems of *The Open Sea* examined here display in-
creased ease of form and diction, more personal voices and contexts,
and greater access combined with greater complexity. In them, the
urges for order and affirmation are balanced and contained by an
increasing inclusion of all that defies those urges and obstructs
their satisfaction. As Richard Howard suggests, these are poems
that question form, yet abide its necessity.[14] These characteristics
deepen in Meredith's next volume.

The Wreck of the Thresher and Other Poems

William Meredith's fourth book, *The Wreck of the Thresher
and Other Poems*, both consolidates and consummates previous
advances, but it also moves off in new directions. In the years be-
tween *The Open Sea* and *The Wreck of the Thresher* (1964)
Meredith became friendly with Robert Frost and John Berryman
and translated the poems of Apollinaire. Meredith himself has
spoken of Frost's influence. Asked by interviewer Gregory Fitz-
Gerald if he felt that Frost had "any effect" on his work, Meredith
replied: "I think he has in making me, in my own way, strive for
the kind of colloquial language that distinguishes his poems. I see

a decline in the borrowed rhetoric of my first book, and gradually my poems begin to sound more and more like me. . . . I learned that from his poems. The other thing my poems aspire to do that his do is to keep a sense of humor always at the corner of the picture." Earlier in the same interview Meredith noted a more general influence, the instructiveness of Frost's "absolute solidity in the face of the twentieth century."[15] Meredith seems also to have learned something about Frost's cunning genre of the seemingly rambling narrative poem.

The influence of John Berryman is more difficult to place in even such general ways. Certainly their work is dramatically different, Berryman's extreme and pyrotechnic, Meredith's more balanced and calm. Yet, by Meredith's own account, they share an interest in "people in crisis" and a view of them that amounts to a "qualified optimism . . . about crisis as a medium of grace."[16] Meredith also seems to have learned a good deal from Berryman about more open, organic forms ("the sense of individual selection of the form for each poem")[17] and about the possibilities of a poetry that might be personal without being careless and indecorous. His beautiful prose elegy, "In Loving Memory of the Late Author of *The Dream Songs*," as well as his poems, strongly suggest such connections.

The influence of the Apollinaire translations (five of which appear here in versions slightly different from those in *Alcools*) is in some ways even harder to pinpoint, but Meredith sheds a good deal of light on the matter himself. Commenting on the tendency of many contemporary poets to turn to translation, Meredith has said:

"It may have to do with our needing to refresh the themes and images of our own poetry at this moment. . . . I translated Guillaume Apollinaire's *Alcools* because those poems not only had an enormous excitement for people of our moment, but they also, I think, were very useful for me. I don't believe any poet gets involved in a translation that doesn't have something to do with where he's going to. . . . Apollinaire's was one of the first really open imaginations in modern poetry, or so I think. And I have one of the up-tightest imaginations in modern poetry, or so I think. So I realized this was an affinity I had found that would be good for me to explore. I wrote some poems when I was working on Apollinaire that started me in a whole new direction."[18]

What is clear from all this is not so much who influenced Meredith to do what in any particular poem, but that Frost, Berryman, and Apollinaire each contributed something to Meredith's own already initiated and continuing development of a poetry more colloquially direct, more formally organic, more personal, more complexly accessible, and in a more relaxed and experimental line.

In spite of these changes, however, and although there are none of the sonnets, sestinas, and villanelles of earlier work in this book, Meredith does not surrender his formal tendencies. An earlier sort of allusiveness returns; references are made to Shelley's *Prometheus Unbound*, to *King Lear* and the *Inferno*, and to the classical myths of Orpheus and of the rape of Philomela by King Tereus. And there is continuing, although more experimental, exploitation of rhyme and, especially effective, of slant rhyme. There are also several poems in a verse form of which Meredith is a master, the quatrain (also, by the way, the favorite form of Frost). Recalling Meredith's statement that his earlier formal poems "were primarily rational attempts to word accurately something I thought I understood," it is not surprising that the most formal poems in this volume are best described as a poetry of statement. In *abab* quatrains, "Orpheus" retells the mythical musician's story in "his own" colloquial and energetic voice. As it does so, Orpheus becomes a type of the experienced artist. He has had his gifts from the gods, has won and inexplicably lost the girl, suffered through hell, won the girl back with his art, lost her again, and through it all made a music fabling order out of chaos: "The meaningless ordeals I've tuned to meaning! / The foul caprice I've zithered into just!" For all the idealizations, however, his song remains as aware of limits as of possibilities: "*Lend*

me Eurydice, I sing and sing." For a living man, even at best only
temporary loans of the ideal are available, no matter how potent
his ordering art.

Despite its carefully distanced third-person title, "For His
Father" makes what seems a quite personal statement—although
with undeniable general application—about the conflicts and bit-
tersweet resolutions of relations between father and son. This is
not presented as drama. The statement's skeleton is more or less
entire in the first of the poem's four envelope (*abba*) quatrains:

> When I was young I looked high and low for a father,
> And what blond sons you must have tried on then!
> But only your blood could give us our two men
> And in the end we settled for one another.
>
> (10)

The remaining stanzas flesh out the skeleton's form, and the
poem ends on the expected, but nonetheless impressive note of
reconciliation: "You use my eyes at last; I sign your name / De-
liberately beneath my life and art." To say that this, like "Orpheus,"
words accurately something understood implies no slighting of its
quality. It does, though, serve to differentiate these poems and
others like them from another kind that Meredith is beginning
increasingly to write.

The poems of this kind are typically less final, more provisional,
and more dramatic in their inclusion of what resists order, praise,
and affirmation than Meredith's more statemental poems. Not sur-
prisingly, most of them are in less formal modes. Still, examina-
tion of them can begin with one that *is* formal, with the fine
quatrains of "An Assent to Wildflowers." With rich allusions
to *King Lear*, to its complex visions of nature, and especially to
Gloucester's seeing blindness, the poem considers the meaning of a
large bouquet of black-eyed susans, "staring out of a bronze
vase." Plucked by beloved hands, one thing the flowers mean is
love, but seen from another angle, they suggest the violence and
destruction that calls all love in question. While never denying

the darkness of such doubts, the poem includes them in its final affirmation: "I imagine the world, I imagine the world and you in it: / There's flowering, there's a dark question answered yes." These last lines might almost be taken as a motto for the major poems of *The Wreck of the Thresher*. In them, as in "An Assent to Wildflowers," the thematic breakthroughs claimed for *The Open Sea* are combined. The theme of order as a moral imperative in a less than orderly world, and an often intense awareness of the threat of chaos in the self and its domestic locales, converge in impressive dramas of the ordering consciousness. Order, affirmation, or praise still typically result, but now the results are more fully tested and qualified by their unvanquishable opposites. Unlike "An Assent to Wildflowers," these poems are often open and experimental in form.

"On Falling Asleep to Birdsong" is reminiscent in title and otherwise of the earlier "On Falling Asleep by Firelight," but it is even more willing than that poem to yield, at least temporarily, to the non-rational. As the speaker drifts toward sleep, he hears the native whippoorwill calling, unanswered, in dark woods. The sound creates bleak images of his own loneliness, of his parents' deaths, of his own fears of death. In an attempt to resist such thoughts, he makes a willed effort to dream of more ideal, foreign birds, of nightingales. However, will is undercut by sleep, the subconscious, and—in a stranger sense—the real. The image of nightingales triggers a dream of the story Ovid tells of Philomela (later turned into a nightingale), who was raped and had her tongue torn out by Tereus, and who, much later, took with her sister Procne horrible revenge upon him. The facts of violence, including time's violence, cannot be erased by any act of will. However, when the whippoorwill is heard again, although still unanswered by another bird, its song produces a response quite different than it had before. Given a clue by his dream of Ovid's moral tale, the speaker identifies with the whippoorwill and from its endurance takes courage for endurance of his own. He makes his own fable, inventing out of the whippoorwill's "constant song" the myth that life "indeed is one" and that, like Philomela, we therefore "will prevail." As does Ovid's tale, now also reinterpreted, his own suggests the possibility that order, meaning, and art might outlast destruction, violence, and time. This is no easy solution. The argument has qualifying flaws. It is, after all, only a dream, a fable. Nevertheless, it may be all we have, and it is something:

> I will grow old, as a man
> Will read of a transformation:
> Knowing it is a fable
> Contrived to answer a question
> Answered, if ever, in fables,
> Yet all of a piece and clever
> And at some level, true.
> (9)

Although far more colloquially and casually expressed, the threats of "Roots" are equally desperate. The affirmation won from them is equally difficult and equally qualified by the very elements of imagination that produce it (and that are now, like reason earlier, a potential source of order in Meredith's work). This extraordinary poem is a long (109–line), somewhat rambling, somewhat Frostian reminiscence of a conversation between the speaker and his elderly rural-suburban neighbor, Mrs. Leamington. The speaker discovers his neighbor struggling with a tree root that has invaded her newly spaded garden, a discovery presented in intentionally exaggerated heroic language, thus setting the stage for the strange piercings of the ordinary that mark the poem:

> Mrs. Leamington stood on a cloud,
> Quarreling with a dragon—it was May,
> When things tend to look allegorical—
> As I drove up the hill that silhouettes
> Her house against the east. In any month
> She's hard to place—scattered and sibylline.
> (11)

He joins her attack "like a knight in his good clothes," and they talk meanwhile about the tree root's origin and the new roots (potatoes) she wants to replace it with, all of this in the allegorical and mock-allegorical guise of questing knights taming a bedragoned wasteland to fruitfulness again. Going inside (her house is furnished in antiques; her Mercedes strains like a charger at the door), they continue their talk of roots. However, although the speaker clearly shares her near-obsession with them, Mrs. Leamington does most of the talking (like characters in many of Frost's dramatic narratives). Her conversation wanders: from what her father told her about a tree's roots' mirroring its branchings, to the painter Fragonard whose trees, she says, especially when the pictures are inverted, look like roots: " 'Think of the branches tossing in the loam, / Reaching for rays of water, the way leaves / Arrange themselves for sunlight, except lacier,' " to a quotation from Shelley which asserts that there is, in addition to this world, another underground " 'where do inhabit / The shadows of all forms that think and live, / Till death unite them and they part no more.' "[19] Eventually, it becomes clear that this apparently rambling discourse is focused for her by thoughts of the roots of her own past and of her coming death, her own return to the ground. She had planned to be cremated, but now wants something deeper and plans to request burial in the small graveyard on her property where some of her "mother's people" are:

> 'But more and more I think of the beech roots
> Holding up stones like blossoms or like nests
> Or like the colored stones on a jade tree—
> That slope was never cleared, it's mostly stones—
> And in the lower branches, a tree-house:
> A box in the ground where I meet my own image sleeping,
> The soft brown branches raising it aloft—
> Except aloft is down or I sleep face down'.

(15)

In this fabulous place of reunion with self and ancestors, her intellectual and imaginative powers fabricate a quirky, personal, mythic heaven, and now her spirited energy lets her return to the real world of the living: " 'Well, back to my spuds,' she said. 'Don't you hate that word? / Yet it's good middle English. Stop on your way home. / By then perhaps we'll both have earned a drink.' " If, as the reference to middle English adds to so many others suggesting knightly romance, we see these questers drink from a Holy Grail (compare Frost's "Directive"), the degree to which such an idea in this poem's time and place seems foolish, and the degree to which it convinces us nonetheless are the keys to the balanced affirmation Meredith achieves here. This miracle of the quotidian is called in question by its very miraculousness, and yet in spite of this, indeed because of this, is nevertheless, and somehow, saving.

"An Old Photograph of Strangers" is a relatively short poem that emphasizes the potential and the limits of art—whether photography, a pageant tableau, or poetry—to redeem the darkness of time and of loss. In one sense, the picture fails. Its held order is inevitably blurred: the people are strangers and probably all dead, and there is darkness which the light for the picture could not pierce. In another sense, though, it succeeds. We share its figures' troubled efforts at a lasting shape ("some of their faces are just like faces today"); somehow, across the years, they speak to us. Another example of how held memory might give shape in spite of the threats of time and space is the lovely *"His hands, on a trip to Wisconsin,"* part four of "Five Accounts of a Monogamous Man." Lying awake in bed at night "a thousand miles from home," the speaker, perhaps Meredith himself, thinks of loneliness, aging, death, and of his hands that have sometimes countered those threats, whether in taking off from and landing on a carrier's deck, in making poems, or in knowing a woman's body. Nevertheless, the poem does not forget that death eventually prevails. His hands have ahead of them only

                          some years of roving
        Before the white landscape of age checks them,
        Your body's disaster, sure to be traced there,
        Even so slight a change in a dear shape
        Halting them, baffled, lascivious suddenly,
        Or folded cold, or feeling your hands folded cold.

                                                    (38–39)

This careful balancing of the claims of order and chaos also
appears in several less important poems in *The Wreck of the
Thresher*. For instance, in "The Ballet" Meredith explores the
capacities and incapacities of art in a parable-like poem reminis-
cent of Wallace Stevens's "Anecdote of the Jar." In "About
Poetry" he considers the claims of exclusion and inclusion, of
orderly but mild neatness and shaggy but energetic shapelessness.
But Meredith's best and most important work on this theme in
The Wreck of the Thresher is the title poem.

"The Wreck of the Thresher" is, in one sense, occasional, an
elegy on the deaths of the crewmen crushed and drowned in the
1963 disaster of the submarine *Thresher*. Like many such elegies,
however (note, by the way, in the poem's title, echoes of Hopkins's
"The Wreck of the Deutschland" and Longfellow's "The Wreck
of the Hesperus"), it has a more than occasional context. "The
Wreck of the Thresher" is also a response to our accident-induced
recognition of the limits of our technology—and so of our safety—
a recognition that extends even to the "safe technology" of art.
In this respect it is Meredith's most profound confrontation and
inclusion so far of exotic and domestic, outer and inner threats.
The poem opens in the speaker's private world. At dawn, he
stares at an estuary of the sea. Although already "curing," it seems
rabidly foul. Worse than any sound or sight of the in fact indiffer-
ent sea, however, is the nightmare of complicity that woke him and
sent him there to mourn. The second stanza is more public; it
locates the crew in the shockingly common context of sudden
death: "Daily, by unaccountable whim / . . . Men and women
break the pledge of breath." This strategy brings no comfort,

however, and the personal intrudes again. Like all men, the speaker cannot "be content with the terrible facts," but is "cursed with responsible sleep." He has dreamed that his own acts, or those of some "monstrous" other self, caused the wreck and that he alone was saved. In the third stanza the poem again shifts from a private to a public voice: "The crushing of any ship has always been held / In dread, like a house burned or a great tree felled." The distance thus gained allows the speaker to consider the dead more objectively, to "judge . . . what dark compression / Astonishes them now." Coupled with the responsible and therefore saving nature of dreams, this finally permits him to join public and private voices and to offer his special version of the elegy's typical turn from tragic contemplation to principled consolation:

> (*Sea-brothers, I lower you the ingenuity of dreams,*
> *Strange lungs and bells to escape in; let me stay aboard last—*
> We amend our dreams in half-sleep. Then it seems
> Easy to talk to the severe dead and explain the past.
> Now they are saying, *Do not be ashamed to stay alive,*
> *You have dreamt nothing that we do not forgive.*
> And gentlier, *Study something deeper than yourselves,*
> *As, how the heart, when it turns diver, delves and saves.*)
>
> (4)

However, the poem does not end here. Having found a kind of forgiveness, a kind of peace, in the thought that the sorrowing identification with the dead which the elegy enacts is itself potentially saving, the poem turns again, now to the contemplation of a principle far deeper, more constant, and less consoling. Thus, it returns to the theme that roots the entire collection: Meredith continues to affirm the powers of mind, imagination, and art to amend experience and to find in and impose on it order, meaning, and value; he does so while fully recognizing that these powers are willful and wishful, that final mysteries remain beyond their grasp. The last stanza of "The Wreck of the Thresher" brilliantly expresses both continuing affirmation and dark recognition.

"Whether we give assent to this"—that is, to the poem's discovered and invented consolation, its redemptive order—"or rage"—to violent response to the world as unsalvageable chaos—

> Is a question of temperament and does not matter.
> Some will has been done past our understanding,
> Past our guilt surely, equal to our fears.
> Dullards, we are set again to the cryptic blank page
> Where the sea schools us with terrible water.
> The noise of a boat breaking up and its men is in our ears.
> The bottom here is too far down for our sounding;
> The ocean was salt before we crawled to tears.

(5)

Against this bleakness all we have is ourselves and "the cryptic blank page," our effort to read (and write—and right) the world, to make something of it in full knowledge of the odds against such making. In the controlled, inclusive language of this major poem Meredith enacts just this saving effort.

It should be clear that "The Wreck of the Thresher" and the many other fine poems of Meredith's fourth book place him—despite a few failures—in the ranks of major contemporary poets. Two important developments have, however, been left implicit in the above commentary. First, in several of these poems content and, more pervasively, tone, although hardly confessional, are closer to autobiography than anything since the war poems of *Love Letter from an Impossible Land* (see, for instance, "For His Father," "Roots," "An Old Field Mowed for Appearances' Sake," "For Guillaume Apollinaire," and "Consequences"). Second, humor increases. Meredith's poems have always had wit, but now that wit (still self-deprecating) more than merely teases the intellect; it amuses, pleases, qualifies, even humanizes (see, for instance, "Roots," "An Old Field Mowed for Appearances' Sake," "Fables About Error," and "About Poetry"). Perhaps the best example of these developments working together—although the former is harder to demonstrate in brief—is the sequence "Five Accounts of

a Monogamous Man," a poem wryly exploring the wildness strug-
gling to persist in even the most domesticated middle age. Here
is a representative section (*"iii: Sometimes he contemplates
adultery"*):

> I had no insanity to excuse this,
> But for a week my heart ran with another love,
> Imagined another house, down to its books and bed.
> My miserable fluttered heart, you understand, chose this.
> Now I am led home—cold, grave,
> Contractual as a dog—by my scurrilous head.
>
>   (37)

To conclude, *The Wreck of the Thresher* consolidates and con-
summates the breakthroughs of *The Open Sea*, extending Mere-
dith's movement toward more open and personal content, themes,
forms, and voices, toward increasingly inclusive and qualified
affirmations of threatened order. As Peter Davison rightly put it
in reviewing the volume, although in *The Wreck of the Thresher*
Meredith achieves balance, "there is no ease in it."[20]

Earth Walk: New and Selected Poems

Earth Walk, published in 1970, includes fourteen new poems
and thirty-nine poems selected from previous books. It is an im-
portant volume, both because of what Meredith's own selection
from his earlier work can tell us about his growth as a poet and
about his sense of that growth, and because several of the new
poems make distinguished additions to the body of this work. A
close study of his choice is beyond the scope of this book, but a
few general remarks are in order. Meredith has been severely
selective. Of the thirty-three poems in *Love Letter from an Impos-
sible Land*, only six are reprinted here. The same number is
retained from the twenty-nine poems of *Ships and Other Figures*.
The selections from more recent volumes are more generous: of
the forty-four poems originally in *The Open Sea*, fifteen survive,

as do twelve of the twenty-two in *The Wreck of the Thresher*. In a foreword to *Earth Walk* Meredith comments on the principles governing his choices:

In making this selection from twenty-five years of work I have represented my early books scantily, as I have come to feel they represented me.... The poems I've kept from *Love Letter to an Impossible Land* and *Ships and Other Figures* are not the most promising ones, maybe, but poems that engage mysteries I still pluck at the hems of, poems that are devious in ways I still like better than plainspokenness.

The latter sentence applies to the selections from *The Open Sea* and *The Wreck of the Thresher* as well. Over and over, the poems reprinted concern Meredith's central theme: the possibility of order and affirmation establishing and maintaining themselves against all that argues chaos and despair.

It should also be noted that, except for changes in the sequences of their original appearances, most of the poems reprinted in *Earth Walk* are without revision. More important, the fourteen new poems collected in the first section of *Earth Walk* continue the tendencies characteristic of *The Wreck of the Thresher*. The complex (sometimes "devious") conversational ease of language toward which Meredith has been moving since *The Open Sea* is often achieved. Personal voices and subjects, while still relatively distanced and controlled, continue to appear. There remain poems in tight forms which persist in being "primarily rational attempts to word accurately something ... understood," while the more open poems are again more apt to explore, and to do so dramatically and provisionally and with less complete *rational* control. Nearly every poem maintains Meredith's long attention to the theme of order and affirmation tested by often domestic but rarely domesticated threat, a threat increasingly, as Meredith enters late middle age, manifested as death.

The statement that the fourteen new poems of *Earth Walk* appear in its first section is not quite accurate. One of them, "Reading My Poems from World War II," dated 1969, is used to introduce the section of selected poems. The poem is descriptive ("The ships in these verses course through a blue meadow / like hounds, the oceans appear to be parks"), and its response to what it describes is ambiguous, at once critical and generous. It notes the tendency to mythologize and stylize, to make disaster distant and impersonal enough to seem pretty or natural:

> The seamen and the fliers in these poems
> ride their craft like so many Buffalo Bills.
> It is a pleasure to watch even the clumsy ones
> spinning earthward like sparks, or circling
> like water-bugs on the cold night sea,
> out of control, low in the water,
> or going under the water, bubbling like turtles.
>
> (25)

However, the moral position that informs the war poems, their sense of responsible purpose, their awareness of complicity, and their compassion, is also noted:

> Even transformed into beasts in a stylized chase
> they seem to be hunting more than one another
> as they ride across this tapestry, one of a series.
> Certainly they have been seen by accountable eyes.
> The dwarf's eyes glitter as though in that whole scene
> he saw no one worse than himself, and he prays for us all.
>
> (26)

Of the thirteen other new poems in *Earth Walk*, four are in strict forms, three of them in quatrains. Of these, two (each rhyming *abab*, each skillfully disposing rhymes both full and slant) are directly concerned with the human effort to give life shape. One of them, "About Opera," considers a highly artificial form of that endeavor. It responds to an implied question: what is it in opera that moves us?; why do we like it? It is not the tunes and certainly not the plots. "An image of articulateness is what it is":

What dancing is to the slightly spastic way
Most of us teeter through our bodily life
Are these measured cries to the clumsy things we say,
In the heart's duresses, on the heart's behalf.

(14)

The less obviously formal poems of *Earth Walk* treat equally familiar subjects. They are formal, if less obviously so, because, while often relatively open in stanza and line and (for the first time in Meredith) without the convention of beginning each line with a capital letter whether or not it begins a sentence, many of them are in equal or nearly equal and sometimes carefully balanced stanzas. Also, many of them, although in relatively unpatterned ways, make use of rhyme, especially for the purposes of closure. At any rate, of these more open poems, one of the best, and one of the most "free," is "In Memory of Robert Frost." The poem is occasional, a frankly autobiographical memorializing of a moment when Meredith met, with a story about flying, Frost's demand for "Something you had done too exactly for words, / Maybe, but too exactly to lie about either." The portrait of Frost's complex closeness and distance, his ability to give and demand, his characteristic presence ("Even his smile / He administered with some care, accurately"), is convincingly evoked. However, the poem is more than merely memorial. Like many of Meredith's apparently occasional pieces, it finds larger concerns within and behind its occasion. Here, one of these concerns is the rewards and difficulties of a relationship with someone known to be superior and whose attention and approval are wanted and needed. Another is Meredith's common interest in the mysterious way fact and fable merge when we know enough to speak the truth, to make art:

What little I'd learned about flying
Must have sweated my language lean. *I'd respect you
For that if for nothing else*, he said not smiling
The time I told him, thirty-two night landings
On a carrier, or thirty-two night catapult shots—
Whatever it was, true, something I knew.

(19)

Hazard, the Painter

Hazard, the Painter is a slim sequence of sixteen poems, published in 1975. It marks a surprising, although certainly not shocking, new direction for Meredith's work. In it, all the characteristics and developments previously traced come together: the craftily conversational voice (here more like Berryman's or late Robert Lowell's than Frost's, and sometimes typified by a finely devious use of jargon and chattiness); the mixture of formal and organic modes (the latter dominating here in a dramatically loosened style); the theme of order tested by domestic, but undomesticated threat; the wry, often self-deprecating wit; and the merging of distance and indirection with autobiography. In an engaging introductory note Meredith describes his frequently topical poem as a "characterization" and goes on to say that "Resemblances between the life and character of Hazard and those of the author are not disclaimed but are much fewer than the author would like." This at once invites us to read the painter as equivalent to the poet and also—in the manner of Berryman's rather more theatrical Henry—maintains a certain tricky distance, extending such personal-impersonal devices as the third-person titling of first-person poems in earlier collections. More important, *Hazard, the Painter* is a kind of fragmentary, inconsequential narrative. Inclusion of fragmentation and inconsequentiality is the newest way Meredith recognizes and attests to the existence of all that resists his impulse toward whole and highly finished statements and the order such statements imply. This inclusion is the major development of the work, again, a narrative of certain small-scale events in the life of Hazard, a middle-aged, minor American painter living in a time of decline, specifically, 1972.

Although *Hazard* is marked by a good deal of random casualness, it nonetheless discovers in its progression a clear image of disorder at all levels of American life: cultural, national, personal, and—for Hazard—artistic. Culturally, decline is everywhere. On one level, the Rolling Stones threaten the "frail culture of Jefferson and Adams," of painters as different as the fictional representationalist Hazard and the actual abstract expressionist Franz Kline. Hazard treats this observation, as he does the inability of a "Yale girl" to distinguish "lie" from "lay," with a combination of serious regret, crotchety annoyance, and—remembering his own excesses with "The Land of the Sky-Blue Waters" on the family victrola—self-amused, forgiving nostalgia. On another, more serious level, the insatiable maws of cash and consumerism replace the American ideal of the new world garden:

> Who were all those cheering on the gray glass
> screen last night, loving their violent darling,
> America, whom they had married to money?
> He couldn't tarry at that feast—when the wine
> ran out, they would change blood to money.
>
> (26)

This assessment Hazard treats with unforgiving and angry sorrow, but also with a sense of complicity: he is comfortable; he has two cars; his driveway is a *defoliated* landscape; he doesn't *do* anything about it.

The obsession with money that drives and degrades the culture also drives and degrades the nation, now in its "late imperial decline." Nixon is re-elected; a murderous war is thoughtlessly and greedily waged in Vietnam; the people, Hazard included, are snug indoors and adapt to the political weather. Things in Hazard's personal life are little better. For all his enlightened liberal awareness and no matter how hard he tries, Hazard knows he is intolerant—of women's liberationists, of homosexuals—and jealous of the success of fellow artists: " 'He is strictly a one-joke painter.' " At times, he feels he is flawed by an excessive awareness of the needs of others (he has difficulty seeing like the cat, that is, "flat," without subjectivity and, therefore, responsibility) and, at other times, by an excessive selfishness:

                    In his studio
            Hazard stares at the vain, self-centered landscape
            he's working on now. It is going well. It
            revels in his onanistic attention.

                                                    (16)

Hazard is also troubled by his own comfortable and orderly
mildness, the ease with which he makes accommodations and
proceeds more or less affirmatively through bad times. Perhaps the
greatest threat to Hazard, however, is age; he worries about a
decline of energy and suffers from an impinging sense of his own
extinction. He recalls the nausea of his fighter-pilot training;
death's currency is all around him: a dead bluejay on his compost
heap, the glacial boulders in his field putting him in mind of
time's incomprehensible extent and of extinction. Perhaps still
worse than this is the daily confrontation with his art. His paint-
ing—he is obsessed with the figure of a parachutist suspended and
falling over a "plotted landscape"—does not satisfy him: "This
is what for two years now / he has been painting, in a child's
palette"; "He has not been to his studio / in four days"; when
the outer self comes to him and "says it is looking for pictures,"
he tells it "it / has come to the wrong man."

These resonances with the culture's decline that he perceives in
himself are only one side of things, however. As we discover a
shape of disorder in the sequence, we also discover that, as bad
as things are, Hazard still hopes. He still tries to affirm, to create
and share in some "godless benediction," to find and / or make an
order in his life and art. The pronominal circumscription of that
last phrase insists that this shaping effort is narrower than the
images of disorder the poem describes, and the poem's awareness
that large cultural and national matters are little affected by the
acts of individuals qualifies what can be said about Hazard's
qualified successes in other areas as well. Nevertheless, in his
personal life Hazard struggles against his own selfishness, intoler-
ance, and jealousy by seeking a cultivated grace in his family and
other relations. He puts it this way, in a lofty opening statement,

interrupted and partly undercut by, among other things, his children complaining about pepper in the gravy:

> We need the ceremony of one another,
> meals *served*, more love,
> more handling of one another with love, less
> casting out of those who are not
> of our own household.
>
> 'This turkey is either not cooked
> enough or it's tough.'
>
> The culture is in late imperial decline.
> The children don't like dark meat or
> pepper. They say the mother sometimes
> deliberately puts pepper on the things
> the grown-ups like better.
>
> less casting out of those in our own
> household with whom we disagree.
>
> (3)

Hazard feels that he is only occasionally successful in achieving this aspiration, but even his failures include continuing efforts at willed decency, as in his attempt to accept the homosexuality of a friend and fellow painter, or in this effort to control professional jealousy:

> The fact that I don't like his pictures
> should not obscure the facts
> that he is a good man
> that many admire his work (his canvases
> threaten my existence and I hope
> mine his, the intolerant bastard)
> that we are brothers in humanity
> & the art. Often it does, though.
>
> (4)

Hazard's musings on age and death are also marked by a wary hopefulness. Some of his strategies of resistance are familiar from earlier Meredith poems. There is love and memory, as in the quasi-valentine Hazard leaves for his wife:

> What you have given me,
> in those long moments when our words
> come back, our breaths come back,
> is a whole man at last,
> and keeping me, remembers.
>
> (28)

There is his admiration for the not-always-decorous resistance of the aged: "the radical old, / freaks you may call them but you're wrong, / who persist in being at home in the world." And there is his sense of continuity in the elemental cycles of natural process, expressed more strenuously here than elsewhere in Meredith's work. Viewing the dioramas of evolution and extinction at the Museum of Natural History, Hazard (in a typical blend of formal diction and slang) considers his possible place in a life-taking, life-giving continuum:

> We descend by chosen cells that are not lost,
> though they wander off in streams and rivulets.
> . . . .
> And grazers or killers, each time we must stoop low
> and enter by some thigh-lintel, gentle as rills.
> *Who consents to his own return,* Nietzsche says,
> *participates in the divinity of the world.*
> Perhaps I have already eddied on, out of this backwater,
> man, on my way to the cafeteria, Hazard thinks.
> Perhaps nothing dies but husks.
>
> (19, 20)

As Hazard's personal life is marked by such hopeful struggle and by limited success, so is his art. Although he feels he is in a bad patch, without energy or inspiration, he labors to overcome his inertia, even parachuting from a plane in an attempt to make his hopeful vision available to himself and, eventually, to others. Winter, the season of decline, sets in, but, with a winning mixture of confidence and wry self-deprecation, Hazard views himself as "in charge of morale in a morbid time," "Shapes up," and returns to his easel, hoping to bear witness to the "vision of rightness" that gnaws him:

> And what has he got to tell?
> Only the shaped things he's seen—
> a few things made by men,
> a galaxy made well.
>
> Though more of each day is dark,
> though he's awkward at the job,
> he squeezes paint from a tube.
> Hazard is back at work.
>
> (31)

On this tentative note, its mix of hope and doubt underlined by the turn to relatively formal but slant-rhymed quatrains, the poem ends.

Separating the images of disorder in *Hazard, the Painter* from its searchings for figures of order has somewhat falsified the nature of the poem. For its central recognition is how inseparable order and disorder are, how random, accidental, and provisional are their interpenetrations and impingements. Furthermore, commenting on the signs of decline first and those of resistance last has introduced a false indication of their relative weights. *Hazard, the Painter* is not a poem in which the disorderly is presented only to be straitened and put in its place by the orderly. Instead, it presents a complex man struggling to impose his own "vision of rightness" on a self and world that will never submit to it, and at the same time trying to make or keep his own recognition of that refusal a part of his vision. Thus, the image of the descending, declining but upheld, suspended parachutist is Hazard's, and the poem's, appropriate figure. However, his painting of it is never, perhaps never can be, finished; life's failings and fallings remain random, difficult, pervasive, and perverse. The systems do not always, indeed, rarely do, hold us up. Even when they do, as Meredith recognizes and accepts here more fully than ever before, they are only systems and always transient, canvases and poems the husks we leave behind. Nevertheless, at least for a time, an affirming, resisting, human spirit inhabits them and, so, "accepting and not accepting," Hazard is "back at work," as Meredith is alongside him.

The Cheer

The thirty-five poems of *The Cheer* (1980) are very much on Meredith's main line, meditations and richly qualified statements on such interpenetrating opposites as ignorance and knowledge, meaninglessness and meaning, chaos and order, life and art, death and life. Their goal is "accurate praise." United by a constant thematic concern with the limits and possibilities of the human effort to resist the disintegrating disorders of time, death, and chaos, and with what those limits and possibilities can teach us about our own public and private, past and future actions (and inactions), their techniques are those we would expect from the recent work that precedes them. Some poems are relatively formal, one in *abab* quatrains, another suggesting *terza rima*, several in regular stanzas—often of two or three lines, and several quite regular in line length and with iambic norms, but most are in free verse, irregular in accent and syllable count, and unrhymed. Their language and rhythms are typically colloquial and conversational, their methods intricately accessible, their material often relatively personal, their tones intelligent, informed, distressed and calm, hopeful and troubled, and their attitudes provisional and inclusive. Ironically or otherwise, they are always fully aware of all that counters or contradicts their apparent assertions of joy and despair, hope or doubt.

The paradigmatic title piece sets the tone of the volume. Printed as an "envoi," here an introductory poem addressed to the reader, it admits, not quite grudgingly, the facts of evil and poetry's obligation to attend to them:

> A great deal isn't right, as they say,
> as they are lately at some pains to tell us.
> Words have to speak about that.
> They would be the less words
> for saying *smile* when they should say *do.*
> If you ask them *do what?*
> they turn serious quick enough, but never unlovely.
> And they will tell you what to do,
> if you listen, if you want that.

(ix)

Nevertheless, it finally insists that poetry—neither ignoring nor overcome by complicating context, and even in confrontation—remains an encouraging affirmation and celebration of significant, if marginal, human effort, of the effort to signify. Just such saving grace, the resistance of something to an always and awesomely present and almost overwhelming nothing, quietly lifts from these new poems to cheer us.

In the opening poems of *The Cheer* threat typically appears as time and change. In "Winter on the River" ice locks up the world, but an ice-breaker working downstream becomes an image of resistance to the season's "cold / and silence," a resistance that goes beyond mere animal endurance, if only from a particularly human vantage. In "Two Masks Unearthed in Bulgaria" golden-eyed clay artifacts resist decay and stretch human time into mysterious prehistory. In "Recollections of Bellagio" the resistances to dissolving time and change are those of imagination and memory. Immensities of astronomical and botanical time are evoked by the dance of the stars and pine trees. These expanses would seem to render the self and its transient experience irrelevant, however thoughtful. But images, the power to perceive and re-create them, and the power to do so in patterns, somehow and mysteriously persist:

> And who
> is saying these words, now that that man
> is a shade, has become his own shade?
> I see the shade rise slow and ghostly from its seat
> on the soft, grainy stone, I watch it descend
> by the gravelled paths of the promontory,
> under a net of steady stars, in April,
> from the boughs' rite and the bells'—quiet,
> my shade, and long ago, and still going on.
>
> (8–9)

In "Country Stars" it is not the persistence of self but of future generations that resists the disintegration of time and change. A "nearsighted child" peers through a window and with her special seeing "puts her own construction on the night." The lights of contemporary life may seem to block from us the ancient patterns of the stars, but the poem reassures us that the young will make new "constructions," new meanings: "have no fear, or only proper fear: / the bright watchers are still there." Like memory and imagination, the effort for significance goes on, goes on in the context of things' refusal to submit to permanent or general significance.

References in various poems to war and politics and to the pollution of urban glow prepare for the several explicitly public and political poems to follow, poems developing themes first broached in *Hazard, the Painter*. Of these, the first is transitional, the best, and characteristic. "Homage to Paul Mellon, I. M. Pei, Their Gallery, and Washington City" has roots in William Carlos Williams's "It Is a Living Coral" and in Meredith's own "Whorls." It pays tribute to creativity, in particular to the construction of the new East Building of the National Gallery of Art (built with money donated by Paul Mellon and designed by architect I. M. Pei) and in general to the building of Washington, D.C., of the nation, of men, of artists, of stone. It begins by evoking expanses of geological time, seen now not as destructive but as the very locus of construction: "Granite and marble, / women and men, /

took a long while to make." As time is made positive here, so is "trouble." America "took a lot of trouble" to make, "and it's not done yet," but the response to difficulty and incompleteness is (as Meredith continues the effort of *Hazard, the Painter* to rescue worn and cheapened language for meaningful expression) delight: "Praise be / It is so interesting, / and lucky, like crustacean deposit." With this suggestion of the making of stone, the poem turns to human making with stone, describing the solid, serene, relatively permanent structures of the past as the expression of "our guesses at un-trouble." It turns then to the contemporary addition to the National Gallery, which, by comparison, may seem "reckless," yet which in its own way has the solidity, serenity, and relative permanence of a "glacier," and which also has a cutting edge. Further, the addition was necessary, in terms of the need for increased exhibit space and in terms of the modern art it would house (Edvard Munch and Isamu Noguchi, among the "sweetest troublers" deposited by time, are the artists mentioned). It is art requiring "knives of stone," "Pink prows," and "hogans of white space"—an appropriate mix of the futuristic and the primitive. From these hints that, however "new" or unconventional, human structures continue time's glacial construction, the poem looks back and forward and accepts and insists on the combination of transience and permanence in all our human acts, a combination that places us and our brevity in time in a meaningful continuum, meaningful at least in its tendency to build or rebuild from the materials of loss, a continuum to which both our living and dying contribute.

Several poems of *The Cheer*, then, resist while accepting the dissolving power of time. The pattern continues in "For Two Lovers in the Year 2075 in the Canadian Woods," which presents itself as a time-capsule relic of here-and-now lovers. Time's destruction is clearly present in the pastness of the moment the poem memorializes ("we were among your trees / in extraordinary flesh / and ecstasy now gone"), and in the fact that the lovers who speak its message to the future will surely be dead when their intended audience receives it. Concurrently, the poem transcends time by having its voices heard in the future (in this and other ways placing itself in the train of the archetypal poem of the genre, Shakespeare's Sonnet 18, which ends: "So long as men can breathe, or eyes can see, / So long lives this, and this gives life to thee"), and by placing itself in continuums of literature (E. E. Cummings, Walter Savage Landor, John Donne) and of lovers ("an Indian brave and his maiden, / a French girl and her man," and, if they "have August moonrise / and bodies to undress," future couples). As its title suggests, the next poem, "Memoirs," is related to this one and considers again Meredith's familiar questions about art and life (see also "Poem," 21–22).

"Memoirs" depicts Napoleon, now emperor of France and in control of virtually all Europe, recalling a supposed childhood obsession with cartography, an obsession so great that he often vexed his mother by drawing maps in chalk on the undersides of carpets. This obviously idealized story his mother, now Empress-Mother, "irritably" rebuts: "Maps? We were much too poor in Corsica to have rugs." There is little doubt that the mother's version is the true one; there is still less doubt of the deeper imaginative truth of the son's willful or invented memory, as indicated by the irony that the Empress-Mother delivers her rebuttal while resting her feet "comfortably on the Aubusson" carpet in her son's palace at Saint Cloud. Napoleon's descriptions of his child-self drawing the map of Europe geographically rather than politically, as a unit rather than as a collection of separate states, and, especially, as drawing it "after his own heart" perfectly capture both his visionary and tactical genius, and imply the achievements to which it led. The point, of course, is that autobiographical, like any creative, fictive lying can be a way of telling the truth, that the rightly imagined "fact" can tell far more than a literal one. At the same time, the poem retains the literal as a humorous and qualifying context that exposes the counter tendency of autobiography to self-dramatization and self-aggrandizement.

"Memoirs" is followed by a series of poems concerned with time and change and death in familial or generational settings.

The best of these is the astonishing "Give and Take / (Christmas, after a death in the family)." Making unusual (for Meredith) use of experimental spacing and of refusals of punctuation, the poem develops the speaker's mixed emotions—the happiness of Christmas giving and taking and the sorrow of the remembered giving and taking of a recently dead loved one—into an extraordinary stream-of-consciousness monologue in which opposed moods meet and merge: the past and the present, innocence and the experienced recognition that death is for everyone, a Christmas wreath and a death wreath, generosity and greed. Perhaps the most impressive result of these mergings is the maturely childlike and emotionally and intellectually ambivalent imagining of the deceased's coffin as a Christmas present to God.

The Cheer's next group of poems concerns death in more public contexts. "Dreams of Suicide" gives the poet's response to three famous literary deaths, Ernest Hemingway's, Sylvia Plath's, and John Berryman's. His dreams demonstrate his sorrow for, interest in, and effort to identify with and understand these others, but perhaps most of all they show his difference from them, his received tendency to the ordinary rather than the extreme, to endure rather than despair. The third section, on Berryman, is the best. Its dream description is based on the facts of Berryman's death—he jumped from a bridge over the frozen Mississippi—and suggests its source in his father's suicide, committed when Berryman was a boy:

> If I hold you tight by the ankles,
> still you fly upward from the iron railing.
> Your father made these wings,
> after he made his own, and now from beyond
> he tells you *fly down*, in the voice
> my own father might say *walk, boy.*
>
> (41)

At first there seems to be a certain callousness here, as if the speaker were claiming a superior inheritance and self: *he* endures;

his feet are on the ground. But the ordinariness of walking and the contrasting implications of flight—greater risks, greater goals— perfectly counter such claims and, with the reference to Icarus (who was also, if differently, guided by his father and who stretched for the sun, and failing, fell to his death in the sea), produce an apt mix of judgment, admiration, and compassion. A similar mixture informs the more fully developed elegy for Berryman, "In Loving Memory of the Late Author of Dream Songs." The poet struggles to comprehend his friend's death ("We have to understand how you got / from here to there, a hundred feet straight down") and to fit it to his own concern with "morale," with what "hopeful men and women can say and do," with what, in the language of *Hazard, the Painter*, we can do in "a morbid time" without falsifying and thereby cheapening the facts: " 'his giant faults' "; "suicide is a crime"; "wives and children deserve better." If he does not fully understand, he does discover something to affirm; the poet's "character" is to "look for things to praise," and he finds them not in Berryman's death but in his life: "None of us deserved, of course, you." His book, "full of marvelous songs," can help the living stay alive: "Don't let us contract your dread recidivism / and start falling from our own iron railings. / Wave from the fat book again, make us wave back." Another poem for Berryman, "John and Anne," employs an epigraph from Berryman's study of Anne Frank and again joins judgment to tribute. He could not grow up; his "decorum" was "only parody." However, his tantrums were "tantrums of enquiry"; he maintained his search for meaning, his effort to mature. The poem's final implication is that his own flawed example can help us grow, as Anne Frank's more perfect example helped him.

The next poem, "Dying Away / (Homage to Sigmund Freud)," is transitional, an intriguing meditation on life and death, heroism and cowardice. Its speaker admires Freud's illuminations—for instance, his revision of death, newly defined as our calling, our heroism, "the *aim* of [our] life." In response to this, he worries about his own "love for the enduring trees and the snowfall, / for brook-noise and coins, songs, appetites"; "The love of living disturbs" him. However, in considering Freud's life, he finds another view of things. Freud, he suggests, "saw that the *aim* of life was death" only after his own "appetites, songs, orgasms," and his family "died away." Further, when his own death came he found it senseless torture and pleaded with a friend for morphine. In this context, love for the "fair world" resumes its value. The point is not to debunk Freud; the poem admires his insights and praises the genius of his effort, failed like every man's, to know the truth. At the same time, though, it returns the questions he thought to answer (did answer, for himself, for a time) to the mysteries they are: "a man cannot learn heroism from another, / he owes the world some death of his own invention."

The last group of poems in *The Cheer*, a series of six marked by shared use of often lengthy epigraphs on which they are often commentaries, extends this concern with the impossibility of knowing the ultimate significance of life or of knowing how to live it, and with our continuing efforts to do so nonetheless. One of the best of these is "Crossing Over." Its subject is love. Its epigraph, the description of the river of broken ice Eliza must try to cross in *Uncle Tom's Cabin* to reach free Ohio's paradise, is a simile for our own difficult route to paradise, for love, for its weakness and its strength: "That's what love is like. The whole river / is melting. We skim along in great peril." The course is difficult, but in the Kentucky of the constrained and real, "all we have is love, a great undulating / raft, melting steadily. We go out on it // anyhow."

Other poems in the group involve the mysteries of human death, love, knowledge, and being; the last considers those of responsible memory. The epigraph for the dramatic monologue "Trelawny's Dream" is provided by Meredith himself, retelling the story of Edward John Trelawny's designing the boat from which his friend Shelley was lost, of his aborted plan to "convoy" him on what became his final journey, and so on. In the poem Trelawny speaks from "late middle age." He describes a recurrent dream of his friend's death, his continuing suffering and loss, his own coming death, and, most of all, the effort of the self to maintain itself and the past in the widening seas of dream:

> All this was a long time ago, I remember.
> None of them was drowned except me
> whom a commotion of years washes over.
> They hail me from the dream, they call an old man
> to come aboard, these youths on an azure bay.
> The waters may keep the dead, as the earth may,
> and fire and air. But dream is my element.
> Though I am still a strong swimmer
> I can feel this channel widen as I swim.
>
> (60)

Once more, the image is one of constant struggle against constantly enlarging odds. It is this effort of human spirit in the always qualifying contexts of its limited condition and limiting world that cheers us, that we cheer.

The Cheer concludes appropriately with "Examples of Created Systems," examples of made or discovered patterns in the world, patterns of both evil and good, of concentration camps and constellations. The poem ends in an ambiguous description of the mysterious complex of creativity, of what we make, its threatening limits and possible hope: "We flung it there, in a learned / gesture of sowing—random, lovely." In this incorrigibly dark and brightening matrix man's incorrigible making "(it is our nature)" goes on.

A Final Word

In an obvious sense, William Meredith is a New England poet. His frequent use of the native landscape, especially its sea and trees (and "its" stars), his central indebtedness to Frost (also a poet of trees and stars), and his attention to questions of morality and behavior and to the possibilities and limits of objective and subjective stances, all place his poetry in a recognizable New England tradition, as does, more particularly, his continuation of the dramas of hope and skepticism engendered by the tendency to at once read and suspect the reading of natural and human facts as types of larger, abstract truths. It should also be clear that the usual critical description of Meredith as an unreconstructed academic formalist is, at best, imprecise. Since the later poems of his first book, and certainly since the poems of *The Open Sea*, Meredith has moved steadily away from the academic mode and toward the modes of the various rebellions against it. His poetry has become more experimental in language and form, more open and (if deviously so) accessible, more personal, more provisional, more suspicious of the claims of intellect and order, and more willing to consider the claims of what threatens order, including the claims of the irrational, the random, and the inconclusive. However, in addition to his continuing commitment to craft and ambivalence and his refusal to indulge in confessionalism, there is a central sense in which Meredith *is* unreconstructed. His response to the potentially chaotic nature of self and world remains one of ironic resistance rather than immersed acceptance. However chastened and chastised he is, however his confidence has weakened, however his inclusion of undeniable threat has increased, Meredith still seeks hopefully for an ordered life and art, for meaning and value, to affirm and to praise. In this, to adjust a phrase used about him by Dudley Fitts, Meredith remains a renovator and not a revolutionary.[21] Or, to apply the now fashionable terms, he remains a modern and not a post-modern. One might, however, borrow the language of "The Wreck of the Thresher" to say that much of what goes to make such distinctions is "a question of temperament and does not matter."

What does matter is the poetry, which gives pleasure and satisfaction not by allegiance but by expression. There is a short poem that expresses Meredith's sense of difficult but possible miracle, of man's effort to affirm against the facts, to answer yes, to render "accurate praise." It is a minor poem, called "A Major Work":

Poems are hard to read
Pictures are hard to see
Music is hard to hear
And people are hard to love

But whether from brute need
Or divine energy
At last mind eye and ear
And the great sloth heart *will* move.

(*The Open Sea*, 56)

Chapter Three

"Facing the Deep":
The Poems
of Philip Booth

Biographical Sketch

Philip Booth was born 8 October 1925, in Hanover, New Hampshire, to a Darmouth College professor of English, Edmund Hendershot Booth, and Jeanette Challis Hooke Booth. "[M]y father taught me respect for words," he has said, "my mother's imagination intuitively made real to me the world that words reach for."[1] He was raised in Hanover and spent summers at his mother's family home in Castine, Maine: "Save for long Maine summers... where I hung around wharf-talk, messed with boats, and sailed to explore some near first islands, my boyhood was sheltered and lonely." Booth was educated at Vermont Academy, in Saxtons River, and at Dartmouth. In 1944 he left Dartmouth to enlist in the United States Army Air Corps, serving as an aviation trainee until the end of the war. After his discharge he married Margaret Tillman and returned to Dartmouth, now "to read rather than ski," and received his A.B. in 1948. He then studied at Columbia University under Mark Van Doren, wrote his thesis on Robert Frost, and was awarded an M.A. in 1949. During these years

Booth's mother began to suffer "the seven years of depressive breakdowns which were to end in her death in a mental hospital." In 1949 and 1950 Booth was instructor in English at Bowdoin College in Brunswick, Maine, where he discovered that, in his words, "I distrusted my teaching talk, and wanted to write down what few words felt like my own. I ... moved to Norwich, Vermont, and there began poems, encouraged (by such former teachers as Mark Van Doren and Robert Frost) to explore my own bent." In 1950 and 1951 Booth worked as Assistant to the Director of Admissions at Dartmouth. For the next three years, he held various jobs—carpenter's helper, ski-book salesman, tutor—while working on the poems that would become his first book. He taught part-time in the Dartmouth English department in 1954 and, later that year, full-time at Wellesley College, where he remained until 1961, first as an instructor and then as an assistant professor of English. During these years Booth lived with his wife and three daughters in Lincoln, Massachusetts.

In 1955 Booth's poem "Letter from a Distant Land" won the Bess Hokin Prize of *Poetry* magazine, and in 1956 the manuscript of which it became the title poem was chosen the Lamont Poetry Selection of the Academy of American Poets (judged that year by Louise Bogan, John Holmes, Rolfe Humphries, May Sarton, and Richard Wilbur). *Letter from a Distant Land* was published in 1956 by the Viking Press, Booth's publisher throughout his career. In 1958–59 he was awarded a Guggenheim Fellowship, which he used to work on his second book, *The Islanders*, published in 1961. In the same year he was appointed an associate professor of English at Syracuse University. In 1965 he became a professor of English and Poet-in-Residence there, positions he still holds. (He currently divides his year between roughly four months of teaching in the Creative Writing Program at Syracuse and eight of writing and living at his family home in Castine.) Also in 1965, Booth was again named a Guggenheim Fellow. This enabled him to complete his next book, *Weathers and Edges*, and, eventually, to move to Maine.

Weathers and Edges appeared in 1966. Booth's subsequent books of poetry are: *Margins: A Sequence of New and Selected Poems* (1970), *Available Light* (1976), and *Before Sleep* (1980). His other publications include four edited anthologies: *The Dark Island* (1960), *Syracuse Poems, 1965*; *Syracuse Poems, 1970*; and *Syracuse Poems, 1973*. He has also contributed reviews, essays, introductions, chapters, and the like to a number of magazines, newspapers, anthologies, and textbooks.

In addition to the Hokin and Lamont prizes and the two Guggenheim fellowships mentioned above, Booth's honors include the *Saturday Review* Poetry Award in 1957; the Emily Clark Balch Prize of the *Virginia Quarterly Review* in 1964; a National Institute of Arts and Letters Award in 1967; a fellowship from the Rockefeller Foundation in 1968; the Theodore Roethke Prize for a poem in *Poetry Northwest* in 1970; and a National Endowment for the Arts Fellowship in 1979. Booth was the Phi Beta Kappa Poet at Columbia University in 1962 and was awarded an honorary doctorate by Colby College in 1968. His books have been nominated three times for the National Book Award in Poetry and also for the Bollingen and Pulitzer prizes.

Theme, Technique, and Development

Philip Booth's poetry begins with the more or less conventional modern assumption that the world is a difficult place and that man is out of joint with himself and with his created and natural environments. Booth does not, however, accept the conventional wisdom that nothing can be done about it. Disagreeing with Auden's assertion in "In Memory of W. B. Yeats" that "poetry makes nothing happen," he insists that "poetry does make something happen. It makes the world more habitable." It does this by building "constructs in it, from it."[2] These constructs can help us learn, in Wallace Stevens's phrase, "how to live, what to do." They result from a sense of seeing as both sight and insight, a process which perceives not only the surfaces of self and world but also the meanings behind and below these surfaces. In Booth's poetry the mode of seeing is, of course, language, and, typically, that language which especially finds and makes connections between inner and outer, the language of metaphor. Booth is, then, primarily a poet of relation and, thereby, of revelation, a poet of the margins where opposites meet and merge and separate, of the verges of land and sea, reality and dream, factual and figural, civilized and wild, the self and the other. (Even Booth's punctuation, his frequent use of the colon, with its ability to connect and separate at once, emphasizes this shifting doubleness.) He writes most frequently nature poems in which the physical world—penetrated by and itself penetrating the observer—becomes an emblem of the metaphysical, of ideas, meanings, and values. These interpenetrations, these metaphoric acts of seeing and seeing into, relate man to himself and his world. However, nature for Booth is not necessarily benign (as it usually is for the transcendentalists); it may also be malign, or merely indifferent. Thus, if it allows relation, it also resists it, renders it irrelevant (a profound doubleness inherent in metaphor as well as the world). Furthermore, being, as it were, chronic, nature wears us and everything away. Thus, as well as a poetry of relation and revelation and of what resists them, Booth also writes a poetry of respect for the mystery and power of nature and one that hopes to endure time's erosion both in its own making and in the acts of making it often describes. As he puts it himself, "Our problem is less to define the world's complexity than it is to discover, within that complexity, some marginal way of sustaining how we relate to it."[3] These, then, are Booth's fundamental concerns, and they remain more or less consistent throughout his career, although in his later works he begins to pose still deeper questions about the nature of self and others, life and death, and about the very process of making itself.

As his remarks about making "constructs" might suggest, Booth began his career as, in many ways, an academic poet. His first book is characterized by carefully crafted forms, adhering everywhere to the New Critical demand for the well-made poem. However, despite a few mildly esoteric allusions, even this early collection is marked by characteristics that separate it from the poetry of the academics and associate it with some of the more experimental poetry of the contemporary period. In addition to their already-noted didactic tendency, the poems are generally accessible semantically and syntactically; voice and, less often, subjects are personal. As Booth's work develops, these characteristics are strengthened and joined by others. His meters become increasingly personal and irregular as he moves toward a more organic, usually short, heavily stressed line, marked by impressive use of enjambment and achieving the grace of laconic, halting conversation. Allusiveness to systems of high culture is rare. The fixed stanza forms of the first volume are abandoned. Attention to dream and memory states increases. However, while these qualities suggest revolt against academic orthodoxy, Booth's poems remain carefully crafted, and even in later volumes, although less typically, they still employ stanzas of equal length and balanced pattern. Although the early use of externally enforced patterns (*terza rima*, for instance) is discontinued, the later poems still frequently employ rhyme (both internal and end rhyme) and do so with special consistency in order to create a sense of closure, of completeness, at the ends of poems. These characteristics are consistent until Booth's most recent work. They are not abandoned, but, as he begins more often to question and doubt his acts of making, he also turns toward freer stanzas, less rhyme, and less insistent closure. There is also in these latest poems an increasingly *direct* use of autobiographical material.

Letter from a Distant Land

Philip Booth's first book, *Letter from a Distant Land* (1957), is a collection of forty-two poems, most of them accomplished short lyrics, "accomplished" in the best and worst senses of that word. Much of it is apprentice work and often imitates the academic mode then still prevailing. Some of this imitation is formal. The volume has a sonnet, two villanelles, four poems in *terza rima*, and many in quatrains; the greater number of its other poems employ stanzas carefully parallel in length and shape. There are occasional attempts at the sort of knotted metaphysical intricacy the academics prized. For example, "Original Sequence" rehearses the myth of the fall. It begins:

> Time was the apple Adam ate.
> Eve bit, gave seconds to his mouth,
> and then they had no minute left
> to lose. Eyes opened in mid-kiss,
> they saw, for once, raw nakedness,
> and hid that sudden consequence
> behind an hour's stripped leaves.[4]

It ends: "The fodder for that two-fold flock / fell, an old brown core, at God's / stopped feet. He reached, and wound the clock." This is far from Eliot or Donne, of course, and is perhaps no more than the sort of watered-down copy to which the mode could lead. Nevertheless, the effort to merge the abstract and concrete, the willful ambivalence of language ("seconds," "fodder," "two-fold," "core"), and the distantly ironic tone all suggest the metaphysical impulse. There is a rather successful metaphysical conceit in "Barred Islands." More usual, however, is the weak echo of Marvell's toughened *carpe diem* that opens "The Wilding": "While crabapple now is a windfall / of blossoms, why wait for a harvest / of worms?" The academic taste for allusion also sometimes intrudes. Not even its fine joke of "young Theseus of Dubuque" can save "Coldwater Flat" from the weight of concocted reference (Ariadne, Icarus, Daedalus, Minos) that helps expose as mere self-pity its speaker's simplistic equation of the city with evil. The Christian allusions of "The Long Night" are equally heavy and forced.

If these often poorly handled academic qualities mark and mar some of the poems of *Letter from a Distant Land*, even some of the least successful of these earliest works show signs of an effort to move away from imitative modes toward, for example, simpler, more accessible, more direct language. At times, this can lead to disaster: witness "big cow" in "Great Farm," "greens my heart at April flood" and "the vernal course brown

conies run" in "Green Song," and "the torrent / of my need" in
"Fisherman." A related desire for frankly affirmative assertions
in the larger units of poems can also lead to trouble, to affirmations
that seem too easy, that will not bear scrutiny, or that are merely
sentimental. For instance, "Nightsong," in many ways an attractive
love lyric, is betrayed by an ending that no amount of echoed
sound, no sense of "prove," can save from falseness:

> I match my breathing
>
> to your breath;
> and sightless, keep my hand
> on your heart's breast, keep
>
> nightwatch
> on your sleep to prove
> there is no dark, nor death.
>
> (23)

The discovery by young lovers of a nesting nighthawk in "Tene-
ment Roof" turns maudlin when the bird flies and the lovers see
"the mottled egg left small: // an unprotected symbol; / warm,
fragile, whole." The concreteness of "Identification" slips on the
vague slither of its final simile:

> Curved windy-free,
>   his flip wings prove
>   the name, and his sea-
>   cry dive like love,
>   flung down the sky.
>
> (49)

Attempts at a harder voice can also be disastrous. "Good Fri-
day: 1954," an implicit attack on McCarthyism, is little more than
shrill: "Denial has a raucous voice: a black cock / racks the
dawn, betrayal's bitter air / invades gray porches where the elders
mock." Its crucifixion metaphor has its own kind of sentimentality.

The accusing glance at blank suburbs and blank suburbanites in "Red Brick" is similarly out of control. Furthermore, there are a few poems in *Letter from a Distant Land* where Booth's movement toward openness of statement is betrayed by artificial form. For instance, the demand of "Schoodic Point Soliloquy" that we "In praise of the redemptive rain stand bare" seems heavily overclothed in the formal dress of the villanelle. "The Margin," another villanelle, also calls its claims of "surprise" and "chance perfection" in serious doubt with the fated perfections of its form.

However, despite its descriptive value, this sort of critique is in certain ways unfair. For even in these failed poems Booth is already working toward the voice and subjects that will clearly be his own: direct, accessible poems in ordinary language made to reverberate with a sense of loss and lostness, of time's impingement on all things, of the excesses of civilized life, and of the hope that the natural world of fact might teach us unity of self and a way to endure. Even in those poems whose forms seem most falsely imposed on their subjects, there is a distinctive tendency away from the pentameter norms of the day and toward short, often irregular and heavily stressed lines, and short, often two- or three-line stanzas. On the other hand, even as Booth begins to turn toward more personal and open forms, he retains his commitment to the well-made poem, retains it, with important late exceptions, almost throughout his career.

Among the more successful poems of *Letter from a Distant Land* are a few marked by humor. Most notable are the slight "Crossing," a clever train poem fueled by sonic imitation, and the slightly more substantial "Ego," with its witty and self-deprecating exposure of a young flight trainee's fantasies of heroic power. The clearly autobiographical impulse at work in the latter poem is used to quite different effect in several others.

In "Design" the poet's daughters "tramp" patterns into a yard full of snow. They are joyously innocent of the facts of time ("the tree / they won't outgrow") and of cold ("the yard . . . will freeze, freeze / hard"), facts their father surely knows. In this fine evocation of innocence and loss Booth touches on what will be a major theme: "design / within design," man's small made pattern inside nature's larger one, somehow together, somehow apart. Personal doubts more immediate and more difficult inform "Storm in a Formal Garden," a poem based on his mother's "depressive breakdowns." No mask or indirection provides a soothing distance as the mother, apparently in a psychiatric institution, is described inhabiting a stormy world of thunder, lightning, panic, and squall, a world of fiery, potentially self-destroying impulse. Against this wild and dangerous freedom, of which he dreams, the son is miles away in a "normal" world, working a formal garden back to shape. Although his choice is hard and impulse tempts him, he chooses order "beyond his mother's hope / and will": "I clear the overgrown / last path my heart must rake." The cost of such choosing, in freedom, in conscience, in pain, is rendered in the felt ambivalence of "rake." In some ways this poem's feelings are less than fully worked out, but its nearly confessional tone, its sense of desperate choice, and its urge to survival all point directions Booth's later work will variously take.

Quite other notes are struck in other poems in *Letter from a Distant Land*. For instance, "Barred Islands" is a fine love poem, conveying sentiment without sentimentality. Two lovers had rowed out, planning a swim off two islands in "a blue Maine bay." They rowed between the islands' "sandspit ends" and then, oars shipped, floated on the high tide that separates the islands and, looking down, saw

> over, over, the tide-
> sunk bar; there where the run
> of current, the waving sun,
> showed clear on the waterglass
> sand, on the seawind grass,
> how the islands were one.
>   (54–55)

The title's "Barred," which might have sounded a prohibitive distinction, becomes, in fact, a submerged connector that makes the islands one, and, for at least a moment, the world reflects the hidden unity of lovers and of love.

Other, less successful poems here hint of matters eventually more crucial to Booth's developing career, among them "Sunday Climb." The poem is concerned with sight and insight. Its speaker half identifies with a soaring hawk by imagining the topography the bird can see. As he immerses himself in the hawk's high, wide, and predatory sight, he almost wishes himself "a hawk's pure shape." However, human sight can never be as purely reductive as the bird's. The speaker knows more than what he sees, and his imagination widens to identify with prey as well as preyer. Thus, he is twice alone, neither merely rabbit nor merely hawk, on "the sheer edge of human sight," the verge where seeing and imagination merge toward moral insight, alienate us from the nature of which we are part, and make us what we are. These themes are treated rather smugly here, but they will become essential.

A better and more central poem is "Chart 1203." A major goal of Booth's poetry is to find ways of enduring the world's dark threats, or, to use words nearer the poet's, ways to sustain ourselves within the complex of the world. One of the "ways" he frequently finds is in the example of men who know their world's complexity through some intimate "local knowledge" that places them in close relation to that complexity and thereby lets them survive it. Such men, such knowledge, relation, and survival are the subjects of "Chart 1203." As the subtitle tells us, the men in this case are those who navigate the difficult waters marked by this particular chart, those of "Penobscot Bay and Approaches." Like any man, these sail by "compass, chart, and log," but in these waters (and this is no silly provincialism; these are metaphoric waters, too) there are threats that render tools like compass and charts of little use and even dangerous: storm and fog, the "set of tide, lost buoys, and breakers' noise / on shore where no shore was." In such a place and in such times a man needs more than civilization's tools; he needs a deep relation with the world. With that, and courage, he can survive. He pilots

best who feels the coast for standpipe, spire,
tower, or stack, who owns local knowledge of shoal
or ledge, whose salt nose smells the spruce shore.

Where echoes drift, where the blind groundswell
clangs an iron bell, his fish-hook hand
keeps steady on the helm. He weathers rainsquall,

linestorm, fear, who bears away from the sound
of sirens wooing him to the cape's safe lee.
He knows the ghostship bow, the sudden headland

immanent in fog: but where rocks wander, he
steers down the channel that his courage
dredges. He knows the chart is not the sea.

(50–51)

This is a fine poem, flawed only by the use—in a poem about feeling one's way with organic local knowledge—of a marching iambic pentameter (this is sometimes helped by skilled enjambment) and of the at least somewhat alien map of *terza rima.* The complaint is minor. Nonetheless, Booth will be a long time working through the paradox that while man must make his maps, his charts are not the sea.

Also thematically important are "First Lesson" and "Letter from a Distant Land." The former is in what might be called Booth's instructive voice;[5] it is a swimming and living lesson, tenderly given. The speaker is teaching his daughter to float on her back. Then, subtly, without disturbing the mood or the scene, the poem expands to include the theme of innocence and experience:

A dead-
man's-float is face down. You will dive
and swim soon enough where this tidewater
ebbs to the sea.

(60)

Then, still without disruption, its swimming lesson broadens to
a metaphor for life, for the poised immersion in the world that
can enable real endurance:

> Daughter, believe
> me, when you tire on the long thrash
> to your island, lie up, and survive.
> As you float now, where I held you
> and let go, remember when fear
> cramps your heart what I told you:
> lie gently and wide to the light-year
> stars, lie back, and the sea will hold you.
>
> (60)

The affecting hesitance of the enjambed "believe / me" and the
unobtrusively reverberant diction of "thrash," "lie up," and
"cramps" join with the poem's statements and its delicate end
and internal rhymes to give what might have been merely occa-
sional a strong metaphorical hold on what is perhaps Booth's
deepest theme: man's need to sustain himself in and within a
complex, threatening world.

"Letter from a Distant Land" is not as near-perfect a poem as
"First Lesson," but its formally atypical, long (162-line) blank-
verse epistle also approaches Booth's major themes. The letter
is addressed to Thoreau, and its title is paraphrased from a passage
near the opening of *Walden* in which Thoreau justifies the auto-
biographical in his work and which Booth takes as his epigraph:
"I, on my side, require of every writer, first or last, a simple and
sincere account of his own life ... some such account as he would
send to his kindred from a distant land; for if he has lived sin-
cerely, it must have been in a distant land to me." Booth's verse
epistle is, then, itself autobiographical, sincerely so ("My classes
are good failures"), sometimes too sincerely so (with some lapses
into sentimentality—"I am half teacher ... / ... professing words /
to warm new minds with what my heart has known"—and moments
of distressing self-complacency). Despite such flaws, however,

there is great strength in the poem's descriptive accountancy of Booth's "own life" in Concord's environs. Besides being a noble experiment in language, *Walden* is a book about a problem and a possible solution. The problem is that "the mass of men lead lives of quiet desperation." The causes of this alienation are a misunderstanding of "necessity," mere rationalism, excessive faith in "tradition," and a failure to attend to intuition and imagination in the self and to nature in the world. Thoreau's possible solution calls for a redefinition of what man *needs* to live, for experiment, for a unifying attention to intuition and imagination as well as to the senses and the analytical intellect, and for an equally unifying attention to the natural and spiritual as well as to the technological and the material. These matters are the context in which Booth's account of himself and, not incidentally, of his time is rendered. From Lincoln, Massachusetts, where he lived when the poem was written, Booth describes his life as "halfway": in place, between Walden Pond and the Air Force base at Hanscom Field; in occupation, between institutional teaching and a life in touch with the land. The threats Thoreau felt in his time he feels in his: the house is mortgaged, vegetables and land are high, the streams are polluted, "cheap people" roam mindlessly "in expensive cars," the destruction of construction proceeds—only its shapes are more monstrous. Always overhead are the jets of oppression and war. However, he also finds the alternatives Thoreau found and offered still available and efficacious: the natural world persists, moral life is possible ("we measure man / by how he lives"), as is unity of self ("I change clothes, moult my partial self, / and walk completed through the open woods"), and the unification of the self with the world ("At home beneath oak / and jet"). None of this is easy: "Man, by his human nature, is not free" and Booth only "halfway" understands. Still, a hundred years away, he is "distant kin" to Thoreau. He is "not quiet or desperate," he hears a "rebel drummer" call, and he answers as far as he can. "Letter from a Distant Land" reports, then, that Thoreau's critique and alternatives are still valid and that Philip Booth is doing his best to live within their terms. This is a tricky business, of course, and the poem is at crucial moments tonally "off" and can sound uncomfortably smug. Nevertheless, in its discovery of ways to use personal and other descriptive facts for deeper thematic ends, and in its recognition of a philosophical and artistic kinship with Thoreau (the latter particularly in their shared "New Englandly" use of the physical as emblem for the metaphysical), "Letter from a Distant Land" marks directions that—with important qualifications (Booth's nature, for instance, will be more often indifferent and inscrutable than transcendental)—will focus Booth's work and produce some of his finest poems.

The Islanders

Booth's second book, *The Islanders* (1961), collects thirty generally short lyrics, most of them considerably better than most of those in *Letter from a Distant Land.* Their subjects, settings, and themes are narrower than those of the first book, but they are wonderfully deeper. The book is everywhere darker, more complex, and more convincingly bright. Often drawing on the lives and facts and weathers of coastal northern Maine, *The Islanders* suggests more desperate and difficult threats to the self and a more profound awareness of the difficulties of resisting such threats, an awareness far from the sometimes rather comfortable, even smug, defenses of earlier poems. Yet its poems are still hopeful, more (or, sometimes, less) confident of the powers of the self (now within fully recognized limits) to resist and survive. However hemmed in, their affirmings are more persuasive precisely because more thoroughly tested.

The occasional tendency to imitate academic modes in *Letter from a Distant Land* is almost entirely absent in *The Islanders.* There is little allusiveness, and that which appears is explained, sometimes over-explained, in the volume's conscientious notes. The language is "ordinary" and accessible. Elaborate forms—villanelle, *terza rima*—are abandoned, but there are still quatrains and many poems in "parallel" stanzas. At the same time, several poems in very short lines and without stanza breaks have a long, narrow appearance on the page, a personal form that becomes a water-mark of Booth's work. Cadences in *The Islanders* are often simi-larly personal. Many poems play off an iambic pentameter norm, with great irregularity of syllable count and much metrical sub-stitution, to achieve the effect of speech rhythm cutting across meter in much the way Frost described by the "sound of sense." Many others use short (three-, four-, five-, and six-syllable), heavily stressed lines to create a related tension-giving counterpoint between the broken movement of the lines and the flow of the sen-tence or sentences they combine to make. These clipped lines com-bine with stripped, matter-of-fact diction to produce a flat, abrupt, laconic speech which can nonetheless achieve deep reverberation, in part through Booth's continuing exploitation of the resources of rhyme, particularly for heightening and closure. In this volume rhymes are more typically disposed in irregular rather than pat-terned ways, but even in the few ostensibly unrhymed poems internal sound echoing creates the reverberating effect. There is, in *The Islanders*, less direct autobiography of the sort apparent in "Storm in a Formal Garden," "Design," and "Letter from a Distant Land," but nearly all its poems are marked by a sense of rootedness in immediate personal experience. The speaker is direct and "unmasked" and often employs the instructive voice heard rarely in *Letter from a Distant Land*.

In a talk with John Wiggins of the *Ellsworth American*, Booth said, as he has elsewhere, that each of his books is "meant to be a sequence in its own right."[6] One wonders if he meant to include *Letter from a Distant Land*, which offers no clear sequence, but the remark is surely true of *The Islanders*. The shape of the book is keyed by the epigraph from Frost's "The Oven Bird": "The ques-tion that he frames in all but words / Is what to make of a dimin-ished thing." This implies, in the word "diminished," *The Islanders'* fundamental assumption that the world is a difficult place without the meaning and value, the unity of self and of the self and the world, that men want and need. However, it also implies the pos-sibility of a response to the world's threat in words like "frames" and "make of" and in its invocation of Frost's example in "The Oven Bird" in particular and in his richly local poetry in general. What we might "make of a diminished thing" "make of" suggests: we might make it out, understand it; we might make something out of it, make constructs from and in it.

Continuing the fact-abstract, physical-metaphysical mode that gives Booth's poetry its metaphoric center, *The Islanders* is divided into three sections. The poems in the first section explore and begin to work out of the difficulties of the divided self in a fallen ("diminished") world. The single poem of the second section presents a transitional metaphor of the shift from loss and defeat to discovery and endurance. The poems of the third section continue to explore the difficulties of human existence, but do so in the larger and exemplary context of persons who have achieved various kinds of knowledge, order, and survival.

Section one of *The Islanders* opens appropriately with "The Second Noon," a poem that contains the poles of threat and affirmation that characterize the volume. Extending the concern of "Original Sequence" with the fall into time, "The Second Noon," based on Cyril Connolly's suggestion that man must have thought the first sunset would bring eternal night, begins with some Adam's and Eve's blind dazzlement before the glare of the first noon and the onset of change. As the day lengthens, they become accustomed to the light and "recognize the original shadows / leaning out from their feet." "Shadows" implies transience and death, but that afternoon the pair ask nothing; like infants they worship the world as self-extension. As the sun sets and shadows "aggregate," however, they begin to grow up, are "Grown tall at last to turn / questions." Despite the moon and stars of that first night, however, they know only darkness: "in that world cannot believe / they see." The poem then ends in statement. Paralleling the paradox of the fortunate fall (the idea that man's fall into sin is what allows him the hope of salvation), it asserts that they (and fallen man) will not see until they "look to," know and take responsibility for, "themselves." Only such knowledge and response will permit them (and us) to endure, to see by whatever diminished light we have a saving second noon in a world gone dim but not yet dark.

Following this "statement of principle," the first section of *The Islanders* turns to several contemporary, often implicitly psychological considerations of knowledge and self-knowledge. In short (usually four-syllable) lines "The Countershadow" half-humorously describes the self's difficult double effort to confront and escape its countershadow other self "that half- / way to the public / light, dissolves / in dark cement." The envelope (*abba*) quatrains of "Convoy" tell the story of a rowboat ride after a morning's blueberry picking. Over and over, on alternate sides of the speaker's boat, a seal (or are there two?) appears, accompanying—convoying—him home. As the story develops, the mysterious seal's mysterious appearances and the speaker's bemused confusion evolve into a drama of nearly interpenetrating opposites: phenomenal and noumenal, fact and symbol, self and other, self and soul. This drama is enacted within the context of the limits of human perception, of seeing and seeing into: "I never saw both," "I'd turned too slow," "I was wrong," "but beneath / that mirror I could not see." These threatening limitations ("my single plane") give rise to dread, but what is possible within them yields delight: if the opposing categories never quite penetrate, if surfaces are persistently mirrors, still much is seen in the "corners of . . . sight"; in a way, the self unites what is in a "single plane." As the amused and amusing tone of the poem predicts, here, at least, the delight outweighs the dread:

> And I, least wise in Maine,
> with double delight and half dread
> flooding two good eyes and one head,
> rowed home on my single plane.
> (18)

As in "The Countershadow," the threat to self in "Convoy" is real but relatively slight and fairly easily controlled and converted.

In the next several poems of section one the threats intensify and humor darkens.

"Mores," for example, plays on "come as you are" and puns on words like "congenial" and "original" to produce a threatening consideration of identity and social masks. The speaker is invited, "come as you are," to a picnic. When he arrives, however, the other guests are in costume. When the time comes for unmasking and revealing the true self and he cannot, the others, thinking he will not and is acting the role of the "barefoot man with a beard," themselves enact with him their own "small crucifixion."

From the personal voices of these poems *The Islanders* broadens to consider other threats to identity. "Spit" describes another social code, the Chipewyan game, played for, among other things, "squaws," in which a man spits on another's chest, the winner determined by how the saliva runs down. The game is a horror, a haunting image of power, weakness, and chance, but in a sense the stripping of the Indians' identity by Christianizing, commercializing, colonizing whites is a worse one, and the game a darkly desperate resistance to selfhood's total loss. That it is played, in turn, for others' selves makes matters that much worse. Another broadening threat, this one including an entire community and, in a way, the community of man, appears in "The Tower," the longest poem (239 lines) in *The Islanders*. It is a symbolic narrative of the building of a tower, probably housing a navigational signal, and of the inhabitants' reactions to the tower in the small town near which the government erects it. The whole becomes a metaphor for the fall from innocence (echoing not only Eden, but also the tower of Babel). At first, the townspeople's fear of the thing is physical. At hearings with government officials they question, will it fall? However, with reassurance and with time (an irony the poem exploits by making the tower the gnomon of a sun dial), they grow used to it. It becomes part of their lives and they even come to feel in the tower ("Taller / ... than any other") a certain pride (the vice that led to the fall of Babel as well as in Eden). Soon, and punningly, "Their original / fear of the fall / is gone." So all is well. Yet something is wrong, something changed

or lost; their world is somehow diminished by some other kind
of fall. The tower's threat has turned on them, turned inward,
and, inarticulate not with the speechful chaos of Babel but with
speechlessness, they can only point to the image of their human
discontent as they

> try to show,
> without words,
> but pointing towards
> the tower, that what
> they can't name
> is, like waking
> itself, or making
> love, not different,
> no, but in spite
> of the Government,
> yes, not quite
> the same.
>
> (29)

As "Mores," "Spit," and "The Tower" intensify the threats
that focus *The Islanders'* first section, so, too, do its next two
poems, "Nebraska, U.S.A." and "The Total Calm," which also
begin, however, to indicate possible ways of enduring such threats.
"Nebraska, U.S.A." is a landscape without landmarks or vantage
points. "Such land / amazes," a labyrinth of sameness with no way
in or out and nowhere to hide. When the twisters come, "there is
no place to go but underground." At first this seems unremittingly
bleak: there is no place of safety; even going underground is a
suggestion of death. Nevertheless, as a Maine man might make
port before a storm by taking the storm's own range, the Nebras-
kan can go to his cellar, "lie up," and weather out his weather.
"The Total Calm" (related to Frost poems like "Storm Fear" and
"An Old Man's Winter Night") is similar, a dream poem in which
snow so deep it buries a house, putting lights, the fire, even stars
out, leaves only "snow, / unmelting snow" "to calm us." This is
death in fact, but even here the ambiguous "calm" and the power

of imagination to conjure up such depths, such "altitudes impossible," to out-nature nature, is its own kind of sustenance. Similar ambiguities of hope and hopelessness haunt the mysterious "it" (death?, morning?) of "If It Comes." If in these poems hope is so hedged and hedged about as not perhaps to be there at all, the last two poems of section one, returning to a more clearly personal voice, move much closer to affirming. "Night Notes on an Old Dream" is an account of a vision of unity with the world that comes from neither madness nor death. More important, however, is the final poem, "The Owl," in which the progression from Edenic innocence to alienation and thus to realistically hopeful recognitions of the self and the world is reenacted. It tells the condensed story of the speaker's encounters with an owl. First seeing the bird at night, the speaker's "eyes blink shut, / but his [the owl's] are full of the dark, / and see." When the man sees the owl in the daylight, their reactions are reversed. Despite such similarities, the speaker is alien to the owl; he tries to stone it off its perch. But the owl will not scare. Days pass. The speaker realizes that by their "different lights" he and the owl are "blind / two ways" to their "different stake / in these woods." This is identification, but with qualifications. As in "Sunday Climb," the speaker identifies with the predator but also with "what's warm," its prey, and, for all this, remains his different human self with his "different stake." Still, there is something to be learned. If man is more than nature, perhaps he can contain it and so be more himself. Therefore, the speaker decides to confront the owl, to wait it out in its own dark time as it had him in his. He does, and the gain is in vision, visionary: "Awake where my eyes adjust / to the dark, I stand frozen now, / and I begin to see." It is only a beginning, but, picking up the language of seeing in diminished light from the section's opening poem, "The Second Noon," "The Owl" offers hope that within the recognized limits of his human sight man might find illuminating light.

The single poem that makes up section two, "The Line," is a transitional piece about the crossing of a metaphorical line, a dark equator of knowledge of the self. Its naming of men of art and action prepares for the developments of section three. There, the poems proceed from knowing to what can be done with knowing, from the making out of recognition to the making of knowing constructs—ways of art and life that make survival real without ignoring the facts of destruction, time, and death. These poems can be treated more representatively than those of section one, since, although clearly a unit, they are not so clearly progressive, falling instead into three related groups which offer exemplary acts of enduring making by other artists, certain inhabitants of coastal Maine, and the poet himself.

To some extent, the opening poem of the third section combines the groups. "These Men" celebrates both the making of artists and the making of men of action, joining them in their shared willingness to suffer for self-knowledge, to "sentence themselves to know." This is, for Booth, a salvational act. Tribute to exemplary artists, both painters, is paid in two other poems here. "Painter" is addressed to Ben Shahn, whose "hands work good" as they work well, whose art has an ethical as well as aesthetic dimension. "Marin" describes the work of the Maine water-colorist John Marin. His achievement is a successful and dramatic merging of abstract and representational, of inner self and outer self, and of inner self and outer reality: he "*saw* how it *feels*" (my italics); his paintings write him into the world (as Booth says in a note, Marin typically spoke of his paintings as "writings," and, among other things, shaped his mountains into the initial *M*):

> He wrote it:
>
> . . . . .
>
> sun-splintered
> water and written
> granite; dark light
> unlike what you
> ever saw until,
> inland, your own
> eyes close and, out
> of that sea-change,

islands rise thick,
like the rip-tide
paint that, flooding,
tugs at your vitals,
and is more Maine
than Maine.

(50–51)

The more characteristic poems of section three of *The Islanders*
present as examples of "how to live, what to do" the lives and
works of another sort of artist, the builders, boatmen, and other
inhabitants of the Maine coast. One of these poems, "Maine," is
general, a metaphor of conversion, conservation, and salvation. A
critique of "conspicuous consumption" in the local and universal
senses, with a sideswipe at tourists, it wittily holds off the tendency
of things to wear out and be discarded. A used-up Ford becomes
a tractor, a Hudson, a half-ton truck; a "Chevy panel" is "geared
to saw a cord of wood." Old engines are refitted for marine serv-
ice or sunk to make moorings. Even an antiquated hearse becomes
a roadside net for "transient Cadillacs, like crabs. Maine / trades
in staying power, not shiftless drives." Other poems are more
particular. "Builder," for example, describes the talk and craft of
Mace Eaton who hand-builds wooden boats in his yard in Castine.
He is virtually one with his materials: "A / stump of a man, Mace
works wood." The stories he tells (our sense of them sharpened
by puns on "lie" and "lying"), and his shaping of a sailing yacht
with memory and eye as well as hands, are merged in the poem
into a single model of the fictive art, the feigning craft that tells
the truth. Mace is a survivor; his time is running out, but "local
knowledge" ("He can't read, / or swim, but he floats the wine-
glass shape / of the stern by unwritten laws") permits him to resist
("hove-to" in his shop). The boat he builds—extending the life of
the one he remembers, the *Annie Gott*—endures the threatening
world like any work of art:

By late May she takes shape: he hums when he
pays in the caulking, and jibes back, eying
her lines, as he planes the planked hull.
His wife died last fall. Time is ebbing
under the wharf; a fair tide and a last coat
of gloss on this vessel, he'll launch a yacht.
Her topsides primed, he touches her, rubbing
his gut, to draw the line where she'll float.
As she will, to the last eighth-inch, in any
sea, designed by his winters of lying
hove-to in this shop—with her lee-rail
dry in a gale, like the old *Annie Gott.*

(54)

"Jake's Wharf," also about a Castine man and boat builder, expresses similar themes, as does "Matinicus," which recalls how physical skill and careful seeing might rescue twenty years of memory from the erosion of time. Several other poems of this section make explicit a related point implicit everywhere in Booth, that it is as much the poet's crafty making as any other that these poems offer as example. This is most emphatic in the poems that end *The Islanders,* especially in "Sable Island," which concludes the book appropriately by recapitulating its methods of progressing from flat fact flatly expressed to reverberant metaphor and symbol, and by reenacting its themes of real but chastened hope for resistant knowing and making in the face of fully seen and acknowledged threat. Rehearsing the terrible history of promise and inevitable defeat on a thin strip of sand that figures the fallen world, "Sable Island" concludes with the assertion that we too must act our role in the ambivalent play of salvation and loss that is the lot of fallen—fortunately fallen—man.

The Islanders is a good book. In it, through understanding and construction, Booth makes much of his diminished language, music, self, and world, and does so without slighting the blunt facts of their diminishment. Its achievements are its splendid craft and its hard-won acknowledgment of a central paradox, that it is, as John

Holmes wrote in reviewing it, by human limits that mankind will survive.[7]

Weathers and Edges

The Islanders was a breakthrough volume. Booth's third collection, *Weathers and Edges*, published in 1966, consolidates its central themes and techniques. In thirty-four poems (again mostly short lyrics—with, as in the previous book's "The Tower" and "The Owl," a few highly condensed and metaphoric narratives), *Weathers and Edges* continues to assume that the world and man are fallen, although these facts are far more often explicitly described here than before, especially in several rather direct attacks on the ills of contemporary civilization. The poems also continue to be concerned with questions of knowledge and action, and with discovering ways to sustain the self's relations with the threatening complexities of the world, the self, and others. Their method of discovery is still an attention to the actual so precise and intense that it swells to metaphor. The location of this attention frequently remains the margin of sea and shore, although there is some broadening of setting here. All this is consistent with *The Islanders*. However, one development distinguishes *Weathers and Edges* from the former volume. It is more a shift of emphasis than anything else, but is nonetheless important. In *The Islanders* many poems offer exemplary paradigms for surviving, often in an assured, didactic voice; indeed, the whole shape of the book figures a progress from constricting threat to contained affirmation. Both these characteristics persist in *Weathers and Edges*, but in several poems in the new book Booth's usual modes of endurance are called into doubt; not even the efficacies of "local knowledge" or an aware, confronting love of place can save the self from loss.

The techniques of *Weathers and Edges* are also generally continuous with those of *The Islanders*. Booth's now typical mode of moving from literal observation and description (sight) to metaphor and symbol (insight) is maintained. His forms are more or less equally consistent, and his rhymes continue those of the speaking voice heightened and counterpointed by the music of phrasing and line breaks. Also continued is the use of laconic, ordinary language that can lift to poetic resonance, often with the assistance of irregular but insistent rhyme. The poems are still only rarely allusive and remain marked by strong closure and by a mix of directly autobiographical and relatively impersonal voices.

Weathers and Edges is also like The Islanders in being arranged as a sequence, although, as the absence of section breaks here might indicate, it is somewhat less tightly organized than its predecessor. Still, it is patterned in one sense by the surface course of Booth's own life as he moves from his teaching position in upstate New York to his family home in Castine and back again. However, the book also has larger, more intricate, and more interesting outward and inward motions. Described somewhat freely, it begins with two rather public critiques of the contemporary condition. From these it proceeds to several more general considerations of the human condition of which the contemporary is but a particular case. After a transitional poem, this group is followed by three poems of personal memory, loss, and keeping. These are followed in turn by a large, rather mixed group of personal and sometimes more public poems on themes of innocence and experience, love and loss, endurance and despair, the hopeful search for meaning and the anxiety that results when the search has failed. Another transitional piece precedes two more poems of cultural anxiety, one keyed by a conflict between city and country values. This signals a return to Maine and a series of poems of exemplary success and, sometimes also exemplary, failure in confronting and surviving a diminished world. The volume then closes with several poems of real, if minor, personal affirmation.

Weathers and Edges opens with rather bleak poems, but not until it has been prefaced by "Forecast," which briefly predicts the volume's working through difficulty toward affirmation in its images of fog lifting, wind rising, and the casting off in "perfect hope" of "the fishboats: going out." But first, the fog. The initial

poem of the text proper, "Choosing a Homesite," is a satire of
financial advice and of governmental complicity in the destruc-
tion of the American landscape. With the sort of wry self-
deprecation that often saves him from certain excesses, Booth also
manages to mock his own tendency to use an instructive voice
by reminding us of the voice's connection to the American ob-
session with the genre of "how to." The poem begins rather gently
("If possible, choose a lot / not already surveyed / for next fall's
Thruway"); however, as it proceeds through a series of caveats
to the buyer (these rendered with witty precision in the languages
of bureaucratic professionals: see, for instance, the humorous im-
plications of social responsibility, of madness, and even of morality
as madness in "Since conscience might, of course / commit you
to a new State / Asylum"), its index of danger increases to include
radiation ("The apple valleys, / upstate, are heavy with milli-
curies") and the threat of nuclear war.

This and another, weaker, poem on contemporary culture are
succeeded by better and more complex ones which explore the
human condition in broader terms. As its borrowed title indicates,
"Heart of Darkness" takes details from Conrad's novella as images
for "the horror" of man's existence. Such horror, the experienced
knowledge of human evil, is undeniably real; it is not, however,
the center of things: "the center is still elusive." There, there is
mystery, as Conrad's Marlow's report, referred to in the poem,
makes clear; there, at the point between what we intend and what
we achieve, the shadow of limitation inevitably falls. However,
the recognition is no more a place for exploration to cease than
was the observation of evil. We must continue the search for
knowledge, meaning, and truth: "what / we need is the poem." The
search will not get us back to innocence, to where, in our now
ambiguous virtue, we began,

> But if, at least,
> we try for some coastal
> station, the poem,

the poem that must
map the bottom
of here, would be
some sort of base
to start out from.

(10)

This image of a tragic quest (the search for a goal undertaken in full knowledge that it can never be fully achieved because of the human limitation that can turn our best-intentioned acts to evil and destructive ends), this mix of anguish and joy, is at the very center of the volume, and of Booth's entire poetic career. "Dry Fall" reaches a darker conclusion. With his "udder-shrunk cows," the speaker inhabits a minor wasteland. He hires a dowser, a false seer, to find redeeming waters, paying him with a dead calf. He strikes not water, but hopeless ledge. Nevertheless, even here the despair seems not the necessary product of the way things are. The speaker brought no belief to his enterprise ("dry-mouthed doubt / is older than five-month's drought"). He cheated (the calf swelled with poison), and the dowser cheated, too. Such negative delusion gets its due. "Fairy Tale" begins with this illusion inverted. A boy, rehearsing every man's innocence and fall, dreams himself an immortal hero defending the beautiful queen of pure good from a monstrously evil dwarf, but he wakes to a world of confusion and discord ("wars in bed"), of ineffective good (his fingers "blunted / with lead"), and of evil that cannot be killed or even clearly seen. It "was not the world he wanted"; it is the one that he had, that all of us have.

These poems on man's complexly limited but not totally lost condition are succeeded by the unfortunate shrillness and flippancies of "A Field of White Birds, Grounded; After a Frozen Lunch in Central New York" (Booth is not at his best in such direct attacks) and by three more successful poems of personal memory and loss—"Homesick Upstate," "A Refusal of Still Perfections," and "Cleaning Out the Garage." The last is descriptive of the stored clutter of generations, although it proceeds to intriguingly ambivalent statements on the claims of conserving and starting clean ("I try to sweep out the useless stuff I still / cherish"; "I try not / to sink in this scrap I dive to uncover"). The garage now a metaphor for the self, the poem ends with a willed intention to save what is "useful" and to purge what is not: "I'm game for different winters in this high summer; / a woman I loved who refused me taught me what I / mean to leave here: *how to let go what won't do.*" The moral and practical conjunction of "won't do" is characteristic.

After a mixed group of poems on loosely related themes, "Denying the Day's Mile" returns more directly, and without release or relief, to *Weathers and Edges*' concern with anxiety and alienation. The speaker is unhappy, "overcast" by the smallness of the corner of the world he can know and the largeness of all he cannot. One response is to try inhuman objectivity, but this is ineffective; judgment will not relent:

> Now
> I couldn't bear it: I can't
> even stand my neighbors,
> or face myself when I go
> to bed with no love left
> from the day.
>
> (29)

There is no escape. Judgment splits the self from the self; time and place run away: "tonight I'm not even / myself: where I haven't been / is already yesterday." The oppression of this poem continues in "After the *Thresher*," its reference to the submarine crushed with its crew in 1963 (compare Meredith's "The Wreck of the Thresher," discussed in Chapter 2 above). The poem is an elegy for the men who died in the wreck (see the moving doubleness of "sounding / their own slow taps / from the coast's dark beer-can floor"), but it goes on to insist that our survivor's circumstance is parallel to theirs, that their condition is metaphor for ours, that we too stretch for release and fail, cannot decompress, that we too "have been sick for months, under tons of possible air." This mood is continued in the catalog of New York City's crushing alienations in "Under the West Side Highway," but as this poem ends there begins a shift of mood. Thinking, perhaps, that his own anxiety is no more than a subjective imposition on the world, or considering the hopeful, if indifferent, continuities of nature, the speaker notes that sirens are, like churchbells, an image of community, that "the sun keeps coming up." This leads to the optimistic, if qualified, awakening into adulthood of "That Clear First Morning," which in turn leads to the strenuous resolution of city versus country themes in "Deer Isle."

Stuck in traffic, forced out of his way by a detour, the speaker sees in an orchard six does feeding on windfalls. The deer seem suburban and tame, "fat and white-rumped / as the drivers who sat in their cars." This triggers the contrasting memory of a lone buck seen once in rural Maine, "equipped / to survive, on the island he'd chosen / to swim to." Identifying with the deer (the speaker's guts clamp, too), thinking of Maine's harsh winter weather and of his own need to strike off alone and survive in a more challenging world than this "thick suburban preserve," he honks his "way clear" and accelerates for home. This is followed by a poem on the elusive mystery of seasons and time and then by two poems that help qualify the potential sentimentality of "Deer Isle." One of the dangers of Booth's tendency sometimes to discuss ethics through the metaphoric contrast of city and country ways of life is that he can seem guilty of a simplistic provincialism, of believing that country people are somehow innately superior to city folk. However, if Booth is often provincial, he is rarely simplistic. First of all, his provincialism is metaphoric, one way of making sense. Second, if he does feel that men in rural settings can be more fully human by their more intricate contact with the natural world, he is also aware (see "Refusing the Sea") that the chance is easily missed and that, finally, it is human response to place, not place (see "Tenants' Harbor"), that determines meaning and value.

At any rate, "Cynthia's Weathers" and "The Man on the Wharf" show that, even in Maine, place and local knowledge may not be enough. Dead at an early age, Cynthia loved the harbor, but "Even here, she hurt." The widowed man on the wharf, sea-legs still good enough to balance him "rolling drunk," is stunned by the loss of his wife, a loss his world obsessively reflects: "Skim-ice ate // at the wharf through March. Like cancer." Reduced to almost nothing ("He pisses behind the boatshed, warm / where his body performs its remaining function"), "The sea is all he can ask." For him, for this much loss, eventually for us all, it gives no answer. The darkness of these poems, as of "Denying the Day's Mile" and "After the *Thresher*," strikes a new note for Booth. In them, his traditional resistances to destruction fail; not even enduring if tragic quest avails. Still, as we have and will see, many poems here weather this deepening threat.

Indeed, "The Man on the Wharf" (who himself retains a certain dignity and courage) is followed by a sequence of five portraits of men whose successful confrontations of threat are affirmations of hope. The "deep" of its title understood as the sea and the void of Genesis, "Five Ways of Facing the Deep" continues the impulse of *The Islanders'* third section as it pays tribute to men who construct orders from the chaos of the world: the arctic explorer Vilhjalmur Stefansson, who used Eskimo survival techniques on his archaeological and ethnographic voyages "to tame not barren lands to man / but man to what is barren"; the sculptor Henry Moore, whose massively chthonic, primal work is compared to ledges carved by the sea; and three Maine painters, Andrew Wyeth, William Thon, and John Marin (the Marin poem is brought over from *The Islanders* intact except for a title change).

A related but different view of making order from chaos is presented in the next two poems in *Weathers and Edges*—both symbolic narratives. "The Sedgwick Boulder" and "The Ship" each presents a mysterious existential object and the intense, sometimes humorous, efforts of people to wrest some meaning from it. As we would expect from Booth, these efforts are presented as exemplary and attractive, the stuff of human nature. But there is more. Expanding hints in earlier poems, these recognize that the

very insistence that the world should not merely be but mean, the
insistence which makes us human, also alienates us from other
beings and things and can lead us to false impositions and to folly.
Such recognitions continue to cast the doubt on Booth's own
methods of knowing and making endurance that is the major de-
velopment of this otherwise consolidating volume. However, if
these poems raise difficult questions about the possibilities and value
of meaning and order, the last five poems of *Weathers and Edges*
answer, at least for now, for chastened affirmation.
"Voyages" presents its speaker in the posture of thought on
a rock in a tidal zone. Like snails, he is "bound /. . . to the very
edge." In one sense, he is stuck there, between opposites (spirit
and flesh, eternity and time, meaning and being). In another
sense, he is outward "bound" for that zone where opposites pene-
trate and where, like the snails, he, too, takes sustenance and
unites with his world ("I breathe as slow as rock"). Playing on
the word "reflex," with its connections to both biology and the
creative alterations of photographic art, "Report from the Scene"
converts the threat of a lightning storm into an image, nearly,
for the insights of relation, knowledge, and love. The evolution-
ary recapitulations of "Seaweed" figure an intimacy that erases
the limits of flesh and time. In "Tenants' Harbor" the poet's count-
ing the cost of his yearly migration inland is saved from self-pity
(as are "Not as Children," "That Clear First Morning," and
"Voyages") by self-deprecating humor and by the realization that
"The word is wherever we quiet to hear it." As it began in
"Forecast," *Weathers and Edges* ends, in "Offshore," in spite of
fog or the dark, "going out":

> On watch for whatever catch,
> we coursed that open sea
>
> as if by stars sailed off
> the chart; we crewed with Arc-
> turus, Vega, Polaris,
> tacking into the dark.
>
> (65)

Whatever new doubts threaten Booth's vision in this volume, it closes with the figure that continues to anchor his work: the human self sustaining relation with a difficult world,

Margins

Margins: A Sequence of New and Selected Poems appeared in 1970. It contains seventeen new poems and thirty-four selected from previous volumes, five from *Letter from a Distant Land*, thirteen from *The Islanders*, and sixteen from *Weathers and Edges*. As its subtitle insists, it is not a "selected poems" in the usual sense, but a sequence. Booth's comments on the book jacket emphasize the fact: "Putting these poems together, I've found that they shape themselves as a man's life might be shaped: not only by the nature of exterior reality, but by images as recurrent as dreams. Or nightmares. Such constellations may argue a limited psychology; perhaps they illuminate a continuing exploration of the world one slowly wakes to; both the world we've created in an apparently careless universe, and the limitations we grow to see in ourselves." As *Margins* is not a typical selected poems, neither is it a merely linear sequence. "Constellations" suggests the pattern. Recent poems are interspersed with earlier ones to form loose groups or clusters in which new work extends, questions, qualifies, or somehow takes up again the ideas and images of old.

The very nature of a book of selected poems signals continuity, and *Margins* is largely consistent in theme and technique with Booth's previous writing. His major concern is still with sustaining the self in a margined and marginal world. His technique is still characterized by rigorous craft and the metaphoric mode of sight and insight, relation and revelation. As in the jacket quotation above, thematic continuities are emphasized in the second of the book's two epigraphs, this one from Rachel Carson's *The Edge of the Sea* (quoted here in part): "Always the edge of the sea remains an elusive and indefinable boundary. The shore has a dual nature. . . . Only the most hardy and adaptable can survive in a region so mutable." Both thematic and "metaphoric" persistences are stressed in Booth's remaining jacket remarks: "I only know that the *I* and *he* of these poems are both me and a fiction, that the coasts and uplands of these poems are at once fact and metaphor: a measure of the hard country where most of us live—each to his own margin of shadow and light." However, for all these continuities, there are new directions in *Margins* as well: a further push into the visionary realms of dream and nightmare, and a few poems that question the very essence of Booth's poetic making. Expanding the increased sense of difficulty suggested in those poems of *Weathers and Edges* in which even local knowledge was insufficient to resist the threatening complexities of the world, of the self, and of others, these ask if the meanings and orders he "finds" are discoveries or impositions, if they see and see into or wishfully, willfully falsify. The doubts such questions imply—the fundamental doubts of a relativistic century—are emphasized in the first epigraph in *Margins*, taken from *The Education of Henry Adams*: "Adams, for one, had toiled in vain to find out what he meant . . . to satisfy himself where, by the severest process of stating such facts as seemed sure, in such order as seemed rigidly consequent, he could fix for a familiar moment a necessary sequence of human [experience. But] where he saw sequence, other men saw something quite different, and no one saw the same unit of measure." The "unit of measure" of Booth's poems has long been typically the relative, although careful one of spoken phrase rather than any more formal metric. Thus, the rhythms, line lengths, and shapes of the new poems are largely consistent with those of the past. However, the lessened confidence some of them express is reflected in their generally lessened insistence on rhyme and collaterally emphatic closure.

Margins' fifty-one poems are divided into four numbered sections, the first of which contains five new poems and eight selected ones, most with upland settings. After the despair of and hope for meaningful life and art in "Letter from a Distant Land," two poems of ambiguous threat, "Was a Man" and "If It Comes," frame the first of the new pieces in *Margins*: "Crosstrees," a disturbingly direct report of a distressing nightmare. A man walks for days across a plateau. Treeless except for the wire-carrying poles, it is a waste landscape, inhabited by blind deer which are stunted and unnaturally tame. He reaches a precipice, seeing over the edge a sunken city. Irretrievably lost, he tries "to trench his way back to known maps or // nameable wars," but cannot; the deer, their mouths "soft as the mouths of sheep," nose darkly toward him. As the telephone wires sag disconnectedly into the infinite abyss, the poem makes no effort to interpret its details, to give them connection or meaning. We are left with a haunting, suggestive moment filled with nameless threat and a strange beauty.

From the relative darkness of these poems, section I begins to modify toward affirmation with three reprinted pieces: "The Owl," with its hopes for a containing and enlarging identification with nature; "The Second Noon," with its emphasis on self-knowledge as the key to seeing and believing; and the love poem "Nightsong." These are followed by the new "Native to Valleys," which combines the resistances to threat of the preceding three (unity with nature, self, and other) in a single poem. The speaker wakes to himself and a reflecting world: "I wake to a mirror of hardwood, // facing myself in the shape of familiar hills." He watches his lover waken and the two of them then move from separate selves to union:

> We grope
> for clothes and coffee, our selves
> woken by waking beside
>
> each other: who climb back down
> from separate sleep
> and are, by morning, married.
>
> (17)

This is a positive response to threat, but it is a rather private, circumscribed, and therefore limited one, as the next (selected) poem, "Denying the Day's Mile," makes clear. There is no escape from the human responsibilities of larger knowing, loving, and judging. That art might be one way to fulfill these responsibilities a new piece, "To Chekhov," suggests. The speaker is troubled (the sagging "rope-ferry" is reminiscent of the disconnected telephone lines of "Crosstrees"); there is much that he sees but does not understand; like the speaker of "Denying the Day's Mile," he has been in hard country and there is much that he "cannot yet love." To all this, Chekhov provides an exemplary alternative. He knows and accepts both facts and the meanings behind them. His art is healing: for readers, it gives apparently random experience meaning; for the artist, it provides a model. The poem ends hopefully as its speaker rides with difficulty but confidence toward knowledge and identification:

> I ride to meet you.
> Slowed as I am by how
>
> my mind drifts sideways,
> I give my mare free reign,
>
> dancing sideways toward
> the Donetz Station: you
>
> will be there, waiting,
> to tell me where I've been.
>   (21)

If "To Chekhov" suggests that the activity of art might resist the threat of human limits, the next two poems of section I, also new ones, call this into question. "Lines from an Orchard Once Surveyed by Thoreau" turns from the social world of Chekhov to a purely private, self-contained one, from the activity of making art to the passivity of a fully open experiencing of reality: "There's no ladder, no word that the bees / haven't already given"; "The orchard quiets; I sip / at its silence, letting the nectar / change me"; "What else / need I know, when there's / nothing to know, save / for the wisdom of trees?" This is presented as at least as positive as the activity of art in the previous poem, and of course it is a kind of knowledge and a kind of love. However, its own surrender of self, and the "responsible" poems around it, especially "Denying the Day's Mile," expose its limits. Nevertheless, passivity has its attractions: sensuous beauty, contentment, visionary self-expansion ("Were I to open / to any more fullness, I think I'd turn into a woman"). In any case, both the active hope of "To Chekhov" and the passive one of "Lines..." are questioned in "Supposition with Qualification," a poem unusual for Booth in its rather direct philosophizing. Its circular questions are these: can man ever give himself up wholly to experience without judging or forcing meaning on it; must he always require "that each event shape / itself to his shape, his hope, // and intent"; is it less than human to surrender to the moment without weighing it and so a distortion of self; is what is human an imposition of meaning and so a distortion of the world? These questions are among the basic counters of modern thought, and they play an important rôle in Booth's poetry from this time forward, but they are questions asked, not answered. As if to emphasize this, section I ends by reprinting "Cider," a poem which both does and does not resist Booth's urge to read the world as emblem.

Section II of *Margins* has nine selected poems and four new ones. It opens with poems from previous volumes, poems evoking contentment within meaningful land- and seascapes. These are followed by "The Gate," a new poem, in which a man "at odds with horses, // asters and women" retreats "from supper into the pasture." Standing there on a rock as the year falls and the day "sinks," he suddenly sees the shadows of fossils lift from the rock. Elated by his discovery, perhaps made lonely by the depths of time it evokes and by the "dead stars" overhead, he runs for the house, "returned / from this field's large history / into the world of small wars." The return is ambivalent. He is brought back to both the realities of domestic battle and the comforts of human companionship. Either way, though, it is clear that purely private personal experience of the sort celebrated in "Lines...," while necessary, even potentially visionary, is never enough, or at least that we cannot let it be enough. If nothing else, such experience must be expressed, and to someone else in the complex of our lives. Ideas of communication and identity unite the next four pieces, the new "Poems" and the reprinted "Night Notes on an Old Dream," "Deer Isle," and "Design," with their emphases on the oneness of the self with nature, place, and family, and of the poet with readers. Still, the following poem, another new one, "Crows," is a descriptive drama without judgment or meaning imposed. Even so, however, its last phrase, "The crows in possession," indicates once more the dangers of such an approach, as do the reprinted "After the *Thresher*" and "The Tower," both of which stress the essential humanness of the search for meaningful endurance.

After these counterclaims for the passive and active, for experiencing and making as modes of resistance, the section ends with "The Misery of Mechanics" and its new and appropriately paradoxical figure of man's difficult place in a world in which action is essential but of doubtful effect:

> his mechanic's
> eye sees that the parts are all there;
>
> it is, in fact, already jacked up.
> But nothing that he can fix.
>
> (51)

"The Misery of Mechanics" leads smoothly to the three new and seven selected pieces of the third section, which begins with familiar poems on "local knowledge" and the enduring (repairing) skill, craft, and art that can arise from it: "Maine," "The Propeller," and "Jake's Wharf." Continuing the volume's tendency to counterpoint, these are succeeded by the elegiac "Cynthia's Weathers,"[8] with its indication of the limits of the local: "Even here, she hurt," and by the first new poem of the section, "The Suit," a companion piece: "even a man who's / lived around here all / his life" is oppressed by loss and the fear of death. Another new poem,

"Thanksgiving," is concerned with the boyhood dream-memory and adult dream-knowledge of another local death and of the threat of the poet's own: "My mother's mouth is grave with snow; / on the hill where she, too, was once young." The reprinted "Refusing the Sea" extends these themes in its contrast of the truly and falsely local, as—in much looser ways—do the selected "A Refusal of Still Perfections" and "Cleaning Out the Garage." Section III ends with "Triple Exposure," three photographic glimpses of self-exposing refusals of self-exposure tied to the other poems by local setting and by their concern with threat, resistance, and loss.

Like the other three, and containing ten selected and five new poems (most of them with coastal settings), the fourth section of *Margins* is marked by counterpoint and by rich ambivalence about the possibilities of life and art. The reprinted "Voyages" places its speaker in Booth's typically ambiguous marginal world. "The Man on the Wharf" ends with a statement of desperate question ("The sea is all he can ask") that prepares for section IV's first new piece, "The Question Poem," with its epigraph from Wallace Stevens: "It can never be satisfied, the mind, never." Like "Supposition With Qualification," it is a philosophical poem, and, as the epigraph suggests, each of its four sections poses a meditative question or questions about meaning and making. In Section I the poet wonders whether nature has sense or motive: "What does it mean, the wind?"; "what tidal will" moves the sanderlings?; "Who knows / what sudden discipline / decides their strict migration?" Section II includes the poet and asks what makes a man a maker:

> What asks a man, on the tide's
> hard sand, to fly his words
> into the wind, with or beyond
> the shorebirds?
>
> (76)

Further, is his making essentially different from the behavior of nature or are their nourishing acts related?

> Who's to say
> if the snowy egret . . .
>
> . . . .
>
> fishes to answer more
> than her own stiff gut?
>
> (76)

Section III considers whether man's making or non-making alters reality's self: "may not / the universe expand / by what life asks of it?"; "Or does the furthest edge contract" if creativity fails? Since

> the sea
> and dune own shape and motion:
> what matters to them, or me,
> if cells divide or multi-
> ply, or atoms constellate,
> with more or less intention?
>
> (77)

Section IV has a similar question: "Why should I care if the sea / is careless?" The "why" he cannot answer, but whether presumptive or presumptuous, reasonable or not, he does care. Separate from nature, "without wing or fin," he "cannot imagine the world / without [him]" and goes toward death, like the man on the wharf, still asking the sea "what I myself mean, / and if I mean what I ask: // *can there be any question?*" Ambivalence is all. Taken rhetorically, the last lines suggest that the art of questioning is itself an affirmation of meaning. Taken otherwise, they frame a darker question still: can there be even a meaningful question, let alone a reply, when there is none to respond but the radically subjective self? There is, of course, no answer in this new version of Booth's view of man's condition; we continue the quest fully aware that it may have neither meaning nor end.

The remaining poems of section IV of *Margins* emphasize, affirm, even celebrate this difficult but somehow elating circumstance. "Sea-Change," with its tribute to Marin's merging of subject and object, is reprinted. A new poem, "Hard Country," overlappingly describes the overlapping resistance to chaos of local buildings. Another new poem, "Labrador River" photographically reports the staying power of local knowledge. "Forecast," "The Islanders," "Offshore," "The Line," "Sable Island," "The Ship," and "The Day the Tide," all reprinted, all present paradoxical cases of the search for meaning in self and world, as do the two new poems with which *Margins* ends. "Bolt" describes the object it names. Cast up by the sea, it is rusted useless, reduced to mere fact, its function mysterious and lost. Nevertheless, in a world so relative, so filled by the threat of meaningless chaos that "the stones themselves are adrift," even so worn a fact as this "shot" bolt may be a clue. The poem ends with man in the near-religious posture of his continuing, careful quest to lift insight from sight, idea from fact: "With nothing else left, a man kneels over it carefully." "The Stranding" closes the book with a dream vision of the questing self preparing again to set out to face the threatening depths of sea and death.

Margins, then, continues the rising and falling action that informed *The Islanders* and *Weathers and Edges*, the tidal sequences of negation and affirmation, of physical and philosophical threats to meaning and value, of successful resistance, endurance, and making that focus Booth's work. In its new poems the threat intensifies: local knowledge may not suffice, shaping acts may be falsifying impositions, death is inevitable, but the questioning, questing self still rises to meet it, providing again, in individual poems or groups of poems, the paradox that is Booth's obsessive center: man must have meaning; he cannot be sure the world either has it or gives it; he seeks it knowingly and nevertheless.

Available Light

Philip Booth's fifth book, *Available Light*, appeared in 1976. Taking its title from the photographer Paul Strand's aphorism that "All light is available light," it maintains Booth's constant concern with seeing as the mode of vision. Its photographic context suggests both his desire to sense clearly and to reproduce things as they are, and his belief that in the process of doing so the poet—like the photographer, selecting, framing, composing—perceives, creates, and makes available relationships that lead to, that are, revelations. As Booth put it himself in an interview: "I think that we all want to modify our world so that we are not merely photographing it. The title *Available Light* plays on the possibility of photographic reproduction which nevertheless involves selection, depth of focus, depth of field. . . . The world is the more revealed . . . from the relationships that enter into the construct."[9] The revelation earned by the relational seeing of *Available Light* is often a dark one. Booth's familiar attentiveness to time, death, and contingency is more pervasive than ever before. However, the volume moves toward a paradoxical and parallel lightening of vision brought on by an acceptance of what is that releases hope from yielding immersion in the present moment.

Technically, *Available Light* is familiar terrain. The poems are carefully crafted and in usually personal voices. Their "flat" language and often descriptive surfaces release surprising and often richly ambiguous resonances. With rare exceptions, their forms are the now characteristic ones: a few highly varied long-line poems and many long and narrow short-line poems in single undifferentiated stanzas or in two-, three-, or four-line units. Their rhythms are the organic, syncopated ones we now expect. There is still much use of rhyme and, more often, near rhyme. However, as in *Margins*, this is less insistent than before, reflecting Booth's continuing gradual movement away from the finished, sometimes self-consciously, even willfully finished, poem and toward more freely reverberant conclusions: "I used to be inclined to . . . 'tuck the poem under at the end.' I'm now inclined to leave it more open-ended."[10] The tendency toward more directly autobiographical poems begun in *Weathers and Edges* and continued in a few of the new poems of *Margins* is somewhat expanded here. Furthermore, in several poems there is a movement, at once counter and parallel, toward a broadening of setting and subject matter beyond

Booth's familiar coasts and uplands. The number of poems on dream and memory states continues to increase.

The structure of *Available Light* is again that of a sequence of poems loosely constellated around various shared subjects, contents, images, and themes. It moves tidally in the margins between private and public, reality and dream, present and future, present and past, negation and affirmation. It ends in a paradox weighted toward informed, qualified hope. The fifty poems in *Available Light* are not so systematically organized as those of *The Islanders* and *Margins*; they are not divided into sections. However, like those of *Weathers and Edges*, they do fall into often overlapping but clear, if not clear-cut, units. Clues to these units and to the shape of the volume as a whole are provided by its epigraph from the existentialist philosopher Karl Jaspers: "Being itself comes out of all origins to meet me. I myself am given to myself. . . . In losing the substance of my self I sense Nothingness. In being given to myself I sense the fullness. . . . I can only maintain my integrity, can prepare, and can remember." It would be folly to attempt to apply this statement categorically; suffice it to say that *Available Light* everywhere involves experiences of the loss or gain of self in response to the world and others. Its poems are often grouped according to respectively related threats of nothingness or possibilities of fullness. Marked by the consistent effort to maintain the integrity of self, to remember the past and prepare for the future, its progress is from the fear of loss and emptiness toward a fully implicated and accepting recognition that self and other, past, present, and future, fullness and nothingness may be inextricably related aspects of every moment and act.

The method of this progress is implied in the initial poem, "Entry." It is "Sheer cold"; snow, already deep, deepens; wind stiffens snow to "windblown / crust": a difficult world, but the poet does not deny it. It is all he has. Nonetheless, he hopes to alter it with his art, to shift nothingness toward fullness, and, in the process, to come to know himself and to make himself known to others. We are invited to follow:

> Given
> this day, none
> better, I try
> these words to
> quicken
> the silence: I
> break track
> across it
> to make myself
> known.
>
> (1)

The voice here is confident, and "try" is properly subdued: the world and the self will resist, but the entrance is made, the effort begun. The next four poems of *Available Light* are connected to "Entry" by their wintry settings and explore the difficulties and, less so, the possibilities of the self in the world. The first two are poems of personal memory. "The Winter of Separation" recalls a childhood season of loneliness and alienation and a moment of ambiguous initiatory contact. His parents separated, the child plays alone. As his mother comes out to call him home, she catches a snowflake on her glove and tries to explain all sides to him—all sides of the crystal, all sides of a complex adult relationship. In response, like the snowflake, he melts: melts in the warmth of contact; melts out of his stable child self into the fluid adult world of danger and change. "Stove" recalls even earlier memories of adult violence, death, and loss, moments then not understood, but still haunting the child now a man. "Dark" brings threat up to date. Its speaker lies awake in early morning darkness, radically alone:

> This is the pure time.
>
> Nobody but me is awake.
> Not in this house. Nobody
> anywhere that I know.
>
> (5)

In response to what seems like fear he imagines those who are awake, each of them—from the nurse concerned for her patient to the gulls dreaming of dumps—committed to time's continuance, the future. This releases a moment of disturbing self-recognition: "I've only begun to see how / I feel, to believe who I am, / to trust what I know." The next line, "It's time" is ambiguous. Is it time that has prevented further progress? Is it time to proceed? The final stanza, with its promised future of light, seems optimistic: "Exactly six months from now, / to the moment, the sun will just / have come up through this window." However, the sense that the self is not enough, that the moment is too much, persists, intensified by a precision like that of a man reciting multiplication tables to fend off terror. The tone of distress won't lift.

The future of "Moles" is bleaker still, but the next poem, "A Late Spring: Eastport," gives a brighter image of coming spring as *Available Light* continues to modulate from winter to spring and now from dark to light, from fear to acceptance and hope. Outside a window, lilac buds, swollen green, are frozen in magnifying ice. Now the fact of time, instead of intensifying threat, signals release:

> by this
> time next
>
> week, in-
> side this
> old glass,
>
> the whole
> room will
> bloom.
>   (8)

So far, then, *Available Light* has moved from alienation and fear toward contact and acceptance. These gains are consolidated in "The Way Tide Comes," a love poem with a beautifully cadenced description of the comings and goings of tide and of time,

and affirming the facts and implications of process without terror or
delusive resistance:

> no matter how we want, beyond doubt,
> to stay the tide or inform it, we
> come in time to inform ourselves: we have
> to follow it all the way out.
>
> (13)

However, such equanimity in the face of time and death is not
easily sustained. In "Adding It Up," a poem rescued from self-pity
by the humor of self-deprecation, the speaker returns to the in-
somniac desperation of "Dark." His random, quotidian catalogs
yield neither balance nor construct, only meaningless distraction
from the terrors of time: the present moment. In "Wear," with
its mechanical images of the aging engine of self that "wears from
the in- / side out," time is equally relentless.

In "Impotence" time seems to have totally deflated the creative
self, yet even here self-examination, the feigning of art, and the
hopefulness of dreams hint at the possibility of regeneration. The
reference to dream inaugurates a series of seven dream poems
exploring *Available Light*'s themes of nothingness and fullness
in a new realm. The first of these, "Dreamscape," has to do with
"a refusal to paraphrase complex perception,"[11] as Booth has
suggested, but it also has to do with a refusal to accept certain
darknesses, certain breadths of time and their destructive conse-
quences, which if they cannot be explained can no more be
escaped. Related threats of alienation, destruction, and death in-
form the nightmares of "Plane," "Attack," and "Laboratory." A
quite different mood is created in "A Dream of Russia," a skillfully
told story of a moment of difficulty accepted and then, through
human cooperation, remedied, which releases a vision of beauty
and love. The central point of the dream poems is not, however,
their positive or negative content. Their value is the regeneration
and the (sometimes questionable) joy earned through accepting

yet confronting and survived immersion in "the destructive element" of the inner self. The last of them, "The Dream," makes this clear in its vision of the diver gone dangerously deep but now ascending toward light:

> If this is fever, I want it.
> Everything's clear: the sun
> has come back from nowhere,
> and brought with it incalculable light.
> This morning will not go away.
> No more will I: I am in my element;
> I baptize myself by breathing my name,
> I give my new face to the sun.
> I smile like everything, even
> at me: I think I am perfectly mad:
> I believe I will live forever.
>
> (28)

Both the balance and the surplus (indeed, excessive) margin of joyous confidence generated by such immersion allow *Available Light* to move from its so far rather private, self-centered poems out to the world and to others, to more public voices and more public concerns. For now, the threat of the moment and of its imminent loss is sufficiently held off for life to go on. In settings beyond Booth's usual environs, the often instructive, even corrective poems that follow imply commitment (like that sought in "Dark") to a future that will come and that may (like the shared season of the affirmative "Late Spring: Eastport" and the darker "Moles") bring gain as well as loss. Two poems, "Photographer" and "How to See Deer," present a poetics of seeing. The former is somewhat betrayed to smugness by its first-person speaker, but the lesson is clear and attractive enough: "I hunt light"; "Whenever I learn to see / I turn native"; light doesn't hold, it changes, but the changes

> balance. Before they tip through
> to regroup I let
> my eye open, fill
> for a fraction of
> truth, and shut:
>   I keep for life
> how light
> shapes how
> lives deepen.
>
>   (29–30)

Although there is no denying the fine ambiguities generated by the enjambments of this poem's final lines, the more generalized voice of "How to See Deer" is more convincing. It advises a patient identification of self with world as the requirement of vision:

> You've come to assume
> protective color; now
> colors reform to
>
> new shapes in your eye.
> You've learned by now
> to wait without waiting;
>
> as if it were dusk
> look into light falling:
> in deep relief
>
> things even out. Be
> careless of nothing. See
> what you see.
>
>   (31–32)

The active and passive seeing demanded by the casually careful, carefully casual final phrase is crucial—as statement and as method —to Booth's kind of making. Similar matters quite differently expressed inform "Strata," with its demand that the "mind be grounded" in the particulars of things, and its further recognition and demonstration that such surfaces, although essential, are not sufficient, that the poet must select, relate, compose if he is to get below surface to the layers of things and "speak / for the planet." "Peru" and "Vermont" exemplify photographic detail made to rise toward essential speech. Another place poem, "Longleaf Pine: Georgia," begins in pictorial description and moves to re-create the image (from "This Dream") of the self ascending from immersion in darkness toward light.

Two other poems in this group criticize false modes of seeing. "Let the Trees" decries our psychological and technological self-absorption and the secondhand (instrumented, mass-communicated) seeing it implies. It recommends a return of attention to the other of the physical world, an attention that will provide us a proper sense of who and where we are. The last line, "*come to your senses*," punningly conjoins Booth's unified sense of perception as sight, cognition, and thought. "A Number of Ways of Looking at It" is a sometimes playful, sometimes serious look at television, presented, like a few other poems in *Available Light*, as a series of more or less connected, riddle-like definitions. Its major thrust is that television's removed kind of seeing falsifies the world and distances us from reality and from our selves.

In *Available Light* Booth's interests in photography and in the possibility and the threat of the moment continue in poems based on the work of two American photographers. "A Number of Rooms" pays tribute to the archival power of Walker Evans's pictures, to their ability to capture and hold the otherwise fleeting moment. Several are described in a kind of exhibition catalog that emphasizes the selection, posing, and framing, the technical decisions that lift them from documentation into art. In another version of Booth's own poetics, his own version of objective correlative, Evans's photographs show relation and therefore revelation. Like certain poems, their images expose "without comment." A different response to photography's arranged and captured moments appears in "Snapshots from Kentucky," dedicated to Ralph Eugene Meatyard. Here, in a dramatic monologue in dialect (a voice unusual for Booth and another example of the sort of broadening that occurs in *Available Light*), art's arresting of time is not enough. Instead of being described in series, the photographs in this poem are lifted from their frozen moments and reinserted in the flux of time by being "tied together in an imagined narrative, making a story as if the voice were telling about them as apocalyptic events."[12] In the process (one related to Meatyard's joining the disparate subjects of his Lucybelle Crater series by posing them all in the same masks), the poem becomes a near meditation on the relation of art to time and change. The distance between a photograph of the past and the facts of the present, the dissolution affecting any construction, is staggering:

> If you get
> to think about how sills rot,
> or about washed mortar letting
>
> bricks float through
> the orchard, you might
> think gravity don't
>
> exactly hold. Not, any-
> ways, here. It's so
> things got loose; nothing's
>
> stayed.
>
> (48)

Nevertheless, the speaker says, this does not invalidate construction; rather, it places it in its properly limited, contingent context:

> But that don't mean different
> than what you see, just
>
> this is the shape
> we each was in
> when it happened.
>
> (48)

The returned sense of time's contingency, however resisted in "Snapshots from Kentucky," leads to poems exploring cases of human limitation. "The Incredible Yachts" exposes a failure of "local knowledge": "none of them / cared to know in truth / what harbor they were in." "Pride's Crossing" (among Booth's finest poems) seems at first a related indictment of the careless rich, but as it proceeds, it shifts from indictment to understanding and compassion. The poem contains a dramatic monologue in the form of a letter from its female character-speaker to an old teacher. Written from the deck of a "round-the-world / teak ketch" that is the most recent in a lifetime of privileges, her letter begins as a litany of the clichéd complaints of the middle-aged, upperclass, exurbanite wife: her husband's *"corporate interests"* keep them apart, their son is expelled from prep school for using drugs, their daughter has had an abortion. However, as her tension grows ("Her script slants // increasingly small"), we begin to recognize the felt particularity of her distress. She describes the order she has achieved on her boat: every line is *"perfectly coiled,"* but the very image of order reveals and releases her real despair of order: will the knotted sequences of life (its lines) ever acquire shape, she asks, and, if so, how will she know:

> *I sit*
>
> *wondering, now, if life*
> *will ever unbraid*
>
> *itself. Or do*
> *I mean unsnarl*
>
> *itself? I know that you*
> *cannot tell me this . . . .*
>
> *But how, if it does,*
> *will I know that it has?*
> (51–52)

By now, the place-name title of the poem takes on deep reverberation.

The consistency of threat in many of these public poems returns *Available Light* to more personal considerations of the dissolving contingency of time. These poems form the volume's final group and divide roughly into those more or less overwhelmed by the threats of time and death and those achieving a certain chastened hope that arises not so much, as in Booth's earlier work, from resistance as from enduring acceptance of the facts of man's condition. Among what might be called the negative poems are "Panic," a series of correlatives for its title state, all joined by a shared sense of alienation, suffering, and the fear of time and death; "Phone," a parable of missed connections and the threat of emptiness: "Again, and // again it comes to nothing"; and "How the Blind," an image of desperate, if courageous, lostness. As in "Snapshots from Kentucky," the photographic memory of "Stations" intensifies time as much as it holds it off: "I guess they must all be dead now." Poems on the poets W. H. Auden and Delmore Schwartz expose the disarray and terror beneath any man's public surface: "The clock travails and spills; . . . . He reads / his shadow sliding down the wall."

Other poems hover between fear and acceptance. "Natural History" is rigidly factual: "The spruce, through July, / dies without sorrow," but the poem's elegiac tone and its insistence that it is only the porcupine that (the verb balancing nicely between "confesses" and "lets in") "admits . . . no moral" implies the possibility of human insight beyond the facts of sight. "Ways" imagines a series of possible deaths, most of them painful or terrifying, but also imagines the limited hope of a crafted response.

Of the poems accepting man's contingent state, two are largely descriptive. "It is Being" envisions the immersion of self in the mysterious realm beyond what we can know, in the indeterminate world (death, imagination, pure being) beyond what Jaspers calls "determinate knowledge of being." It is a threatening world, "beyond beacons," "beyond relief," but if—like Coleridge's mariner —we can learn to bless what is within the deep, we may earn a kind of release. "Old Poem" (its title taken in part, perhaps, from its renewed use of the setting of the early "Barred Islands") narrates the preparations for a journey into that enigmatic beyond. "Watch" advises an admission of death's fact beyond delusive resistance ("the lies / we devise to live by") and promises in return contentment beyond despair. In "Graffito," the acceptance of time and process produces still more: release ("Letting go") from fear ("afraid I / might die") into joy ("I felt the whole stall dance").

Two of the final poems of *Available Light* bring its major movements full circle. "Strip" employs the single-sided band of the Möbius strip to depict the fundamental oneness of self and other, timelessness and time. "Moment" achieves the immersion in the present that "Dark" so feared and struggled to escape. The sting of transiency eased, the moment blooms, like honey on the tongue. It ends with its own Möbius strip, a refusal of punctuation (allowing us to read and not read a period after "remember") that unifies the concurrent discontinuity and continuity of time in a paradoxical whole:

> the present
> gives itself up:
> the past cannot
> remember the future
> does not yet know.
> (77)

Time separates the self from its self, from others, from the world. It joins them, too.

Booth himself has said that the progress from resistance to knowing acceptance of the immediate that occurs between "Dark" and "Moment" "accurately measures" the curve of *Available Light*,[13] and surely the book might neatly have closed here. Instead, appropriately, it opens again to life's contingency. Its last poem is, for Booth, a dramatic departure in form. "Lives" is unusually long (over 200 lines), uses both short and long loose lines, and creates

rhythmic and juxtapositional effects by disposing words and
phrases in the space of the page in the manner of, say, William
Carlos Williams or Charles Olson. Its unusually random form re-
flects its unusually random content, as if Booth were reaching out
to contain more of the complexities of life than *Available Light*
has yet revealed, more than his usually stripped forms and meth-
ods can hold. "Lives" presents a sequence of fragmentary moments
of recalled events of life and death, united only by the recalling
consciousness. It ends, in a beautiful passage about two lovers
skating in a frozen marsh, in full awareness of how the fragments
of life escape us and our ordering urge. Its expressions of that
awareness might be mottoes for Booth's career:

> We slide a foot toward what an old man wrote
> the week before he died:
> *we live, we have*
>   *to live, on*
>   *insufficient*
> *evidence.*
> . . . .
> It's true:
>   *we never know*
>   *a life*
>   *enough*. . . .
>   (83)

However, this acceptance of limits toward which *Available Light*
has moved is no stopping place either. Having broadened his inclu-
sive grasp, Booth—as at the end of each of his books—sets out
again, for he remains a poet of action, of the continual quest to
confront nothingness and know it, too, as fullness:

> opening ourselves
> between ninetails and snow
>   we come close
>   and hug:
>   lives

        we barely know, lives
                    we keep wanting
    to know.

                                    (84)

Lives we want, knowing we cannot, to have and hold, to know,
to know us: these duplicities of relation and revelation are the
sign of Booth's enlarging reach.

Before Sleep

Like much of *Available Light*, *Before Sleep* (1980) is a book
about and responding to human limits, the effects of time and death
on all we are and do and especially on our efforts to know the
self and others and to accept the facts of our contingent condition.
Its attitude is the double one that has long informed Booth's
career: *"No matter how I feel, / I am of several minds."* The
poems move and sometimes balance between the poles of fear
and hope, fact and dream, nothingness and fullness, and they some-
times merge them in a unit paradoxically double.
    The major technical development of *Before Sleep* is a formal
one. At least since *The Islanders*, Booth's metric has been a per-
sonal, organic, relativistic one, as much off beat as on, but the
shapes that metric produced were relatively closed and constant
until the opening out of "Lives," the last poem of *Available Light*.
Closed poems persist here, although there are perhaps more long-
line poems than before. More important, however, many poems
in *Before Sleep* exploit the possibilities of disposing words and
phrases in the space of the page first explored in "Lives." In ad-
dition to its visual, rhythmic, and juxtapositional advantages, and
the greater inclusion it permits, this also allows Booth to maintain
his concern with syncopation and to combine the short- and long-
line urges previously kept separate in his poems, to let the line
expand and contract organically with the movement and mood
of the poem. Like the Adams epigraph to *Margins*, the versifica-
tion implies the uncertainty of measurement in our world.[14]

As this formal "loosening" suggests, *Before Sleep* continues Booth's withdrawal from insistent closure and from the rhyme that often went with it. As Booth's always have, but now more completely, these poems take their resonance from line movement, from dramatic and narrative structure, and from the ambivalence he everywhere finds in and draws from language apparently ordinary and flat, draws from especially by manipulating syntax and line breaks. The direct use of autobiographical material also continues, and there are still many objective poems about other people and the natural world into which the poet-speaker does not *obviously* enter: the mix is by now familiar; the proportions vary. Several poems concern that mysterious realm beyond determinate knowing, and there is a general return to local material after the geographical broadenings of *Available Light*.

Like all of Booth's books since *The Islanders*, *Before Sleep* is carefully organized so that the "several minds" of its poems comment on and qualify one another. However, although it often falls into clusters of related poems (four centered on the room where the poet lives and works, three on Booth's Castine literary relations, three more on the regenerative powers of imagination, and so on), and although there is a general shifting toward affirmation, *Before Sleep* is perhaps not so clearly a sequence as earlier volumes. For throughout it reveals a general, and double, consistency of effort and attitude as the poet struggles to do what he cannot do: to know himself, the world, and others, to know how to live knowing everything dies. However, irregularly dispersed through the text is a series of italicized, untitled poems, collectively called "Night Notes." Directly or indirectly, these sometimes underline, sometimes subvert, but more especially provide a constant context for the poems around them, stressing again and again the complex background of facts against which the despairs, efforts, and hopes of the other poems go on. The "Night Notes" are united by their nearly uniform use of the word *nothing* and by their fine exploitation (although there are perhaps a few too many of them to sustain this consistency) of its common meaning of "no thing" and of its more substantive sense of nothingness, meaninglessness, the void (compare Frost's "Desert Places"). This exploitation is typically ironic, sometimes subversive, sometimes paradoxical. For instance, in the first of four "Night Notes" dispersed throughout the text but when taken together forming a single narrative, the following exchange takes place between the punningly named Noam, seriously injured in a freakish accident which killed his wife, and his nurse:

> Don't worry, *she said*, you're going
> to be all right. Nothing
> is going to happen.
> I know, *Noam said*, it already has.
>
> (8)

Or, in another of the four, "I tell you it's nothing, / nothing is all." In other "Night Notes" the ambivalences of "nothing" are more directly philosophical: "*Nothing is given. / Nothing is unforgiving*"; or "*Nothing is more than / simple absence*"; or "*Nothing has meaning. / Nothing means what / it says.*"

Against the paradoxes of meaning and non-meaning, of hope and despair in such lines, against their choral background, the other poems of *Before Sleep* take place. The book opens with a credo, a wisely distanced self-portrait of what the poet would achieve:

> He has sorted life out;
> he feels moved to say all of it,
> most of it all. He tries
> to come close, he keeps
> coming close: he has
> gathered himself
> in order not
> to tell
> lies.
>
> (1)

There is nothing smug in this. Succeeding poems recognize the difficulties involved: "I can feel, / I can name, what I have to decide: I mean / if I mean to revise my whole life." In "Falling Apart" dissolving time threatens the self. "Flinching" defines a self alienated from its self ("he feels animals in him eat at their reins"), from the world ("Marooned"), and from others ("Distrusting the natives"). However, vision remains possible, as the staying windows, the means of sight, of "Falling Apart" imply. Thus, in "Out of the Ordinary" joy (or perhaps only the possibility of it) arises from the exhausted and quotidian, arises "Out of the ordinary": "he looked and looked / for the joy of it."

This ebb and flood of assertion and negation, affirmation and fear is repeated throughout *Before Sleep*. To catalog, "Matter" is a blunt statement of transiency. "A Slow Breaker" depicts our continuing effort to know by mind and eye the mysterious world: "what we thought to / look into, . . . and we / cannot see through." "Recall" describes an effort to rescue the self from time by accepting its connections with the dreams of a parental past. "A Vespertide" is a time-lapse still life of the timeless flow of overwhelming time. "Fog" figures the self's predicament (its having to live on "insufficient evidence") and its questing response to that predicament. Rowing in fog, "where measure is lost," "I sit facing backwards, / pulling myself slowly / toward the life I'm still trying to get at." In "Rates" images of immediacy and timelessness are juxtaposed with the supposedly eternal names of great men of science, art, religion, and philosophy to imply that time engulfs us all, although at different rates: one for forsythia, one for the white dwarf in M-101, "dead / before history was born," another for ordinary men, yet another for genius. The related "Middling" evokes the terrors of middle age, of man stuck between birth and growing and decline and death. "Dragging" shifts again toward hope in another parable of contingent quest, as does "Here" with its fine paradox of human choice in a world we never chose: we live as if "we could choose / as if / there were choice." However, such balance cannot always be maintained and succeeding poems fall back in the direction of despair. In "Calendar" a woman is destroyed by illness and madness; in "Ossipee: November" an indifferent world locks up a crashed small plane till too-late spring; meanwhile, in the "Night Notes" Noam has taken his life. The falling-rising-falling pattern continues. In "Sorting It Out" a widower struggles with his loss. In "Wonder" the evolutionary power of imagination to recognize the complexities of self might even redeem the past and bring about the future: "we toss guesses / out before us, dreaming to survive / who so far we've become." Although the pattern continues, however, from roughly this point on in *Before Sleep*, there is a general shifting toward acceptance and affirmation. Not that the poems become in any sense at ease or optimistic; they remain fully implicated in the contingent facts of human weakness, of time and death, but in recognizing and accepting threat they now more often, more consistently, earn and achieve a qualified hope. "Mary's, After Dinner" (Mary is the writer Mary McCarthy; she owns the house next door to Booth's in Maine) celebrates a moment, knowing well it was only a moment and perhaps a falsely induced one at that, when intellect and language enriched life with value and sense. "Thinking About Hannah Arendt" pays elegiac tribute to the meaningful life of experience, imagination, and mind of the political philosopher whom Booth met when she visited McCarthy and her husband.

The best poem of this group, though, is "This Day After Yesterday," an elegy for Robert Lowell, who for several summers lived and wrote in Castine.[15] It begins with the suggestion, conventional in pastoral elegy, that nature reflects his death, but quickly, although only in part, withdraws from it, partially because of Booth's sense of what Lowell's scathing critical intelligence would have to say of such a conception. It shifts to a memory of their last parting and introduces the comparison of Lowell to Ulysses that is continued throughout the poem. Honoring his poet's skill and suffering, Booth mourns the loss of Lowell's "collected life," his "unrevisable last poem," and outlines his complex self: cruelty and compassion, sanity and madness, weakness and courage. He then turns briefly to a more general sense of time's universal decay and returns to consider his own relation to Lowell. Booth's honesty is a moving tribute, his sense of loss complicated by awareness of the difficulty of having a master in the backyard, by the inspiring and irritating ("maddening") challenge of Lowell's presence, and perhaps by his sense of the limits of his own attainment compared with Lowell's:

> More
> in misery than love,
>
> I have your life
> by heart. Without you,
>
> I am easier and less.
>
> (53–54)

As Booth recognizes the image of his own mortality in Lowell's death, he wishes to return to the natural portents (seals, heron, a meteor) of the poem's beginning, and does, in spite of his refusal to. The poem then closes with an Odyssean image of the hero finally home and a prayer for the lightening of his spirit, winning its testament of respect and love from wasting time and from its admitted complex of jealousy and threat.

Several succeeding poems strive for and achieve still further release in acceptance and affirmation. "Gathering Greens" dramatizes the effort to survive by assenting to things as they are. Its shift from accepted immersion in darkness toward light, therefore toward light, is intensified by the fact that it is darkness itself combined with light ("shadow") that points the way out, a figure familiar from such poems in *Available Light* as "This Dream" and "Longleaf Pine: Georgia." Engaged in the activity the title describes, the speaker pushes deep into woods, to where the suggestively "old dark / spends the night." Disturbed, he struggles to still himself to accept and endure his circumstance:

> I try
> to learn with
> myself to be
>
> gentle: to wait
> until light
> for the first
>
> shadow to
> point me out
> to the coast.
>
> (57)

"Continuum" suggests that the seeming separateness of things and selves, the relativity of limited seeing, is made in some sense one through relation (now implying connection and "exchanging views" as well as disconnecting subjectivity). If we see the world and others in terms of ourselves, we also see ourselves in terms of, in relation to, the world and others. If perception is limited, we can exchange perspectives, lessening limits and becoming part of a single continuum of being and seeing in the light of the "absolute / sun."

"Thoreau Near Home" presents an example of such shared seeking along a continuum unbroken by time. The poem imaginatively recounts a visit by Thoreau to Castine (Thoreau did, in fact, stop in Castine on his May 1839 tour in search of a teaching position), his acceptance of life's essential contingency ("All answers / being in the future"), and his search into other lives for the pace of life, for ways of life. This search Booth continues, even in his searching out of another's life in the poem itself. He is further connected with Thoreau by shared place and by his (Booth's) ancestor Philip Hooke who, as a boy, is said to have shown Thoreau Castine's Fort George. Assent to a related continuum informs "The Valley Road," where children rise from rotted houses and farms as arbutus lifts from winter into spring. Another constellation of poems in *Before Sleep* is united by another kind of affirmation, Booth's familiar celebration of the power of local knowledge, expressed in craft, to create enduring work. "Tools" joins the working of wood with the working of words, both wedging "To get a handle on how / the day may work," both hoping, by evening, for something—fact or dream, understanding or hope, object or idea—"to / show for" their labor, something to "name what shape // day took, or / one may still imagine." "Eaton's Boatyard" celebrates the ability of the craftsman, boatbuilder or poem builder, to find in the "culch" of his shop or the chaos of life in the world "the requisite tool," what is needed to make things "shape up." The searching, assenting use of what is gives rise to what—a boat, a poem—will suffice: "to make of what's here / what has to be made / to make do." The doubleness, the torque, applied to "made" by its placement, by the line break that follows, exemplifies Booth's own craft in these poems. A third poem honoring the sustaining possibilities of skillful making is "Building Her," where, if the wood built into a boat is well enough known and worked, if its generous assent ("wood gives") is generously assented to, "the hull will / take to sea the way the tree knew wind," what is made will be one with the world.

As these affirmations, arising as they do from aware acceptance of life's contingent dependencies, come to characterize *Before Sleep*'s later titled poems, a related modification is taking place in the untitled "Night Notes." In spite of their ambivalence, until late in the book these poems tilt slightly toward the darker view of things: from the nurse's assertion of comfort toward Noam's recognition of the void. However, from roughly this point on, they also begin to seek the acceptance of the world's givens that might release relief. A series of quotations from the last three "Night Notes" will demonstrate the process:

Nothing is infinite absence
. . . .
the emptying-out of self
I cannot avoid, the void
of not being I cannot
learn to believe in.
(70–71)

The question
is not how to outlive
life, but how
—in the time we're
possessed by—to face
the raw beauty of being.
(73)

I let love wake me:
I extend myself to
every reflection, as
I have to, to feel for
the planet: nowhere
better, with nothing
to lose, than here
to give thanks
life takes place.
(75)

It is still "reflection," the merging of seeing and thought, sight and insight, that fuels such acceptance, that makes its passivity active, a going out.

If *Before Sleep* moves toward affirmation, it also comes full circle, closing with three poems richly paradoxed. "Soundings" considers time and change. Change breaks promises (promises, our knowing so confused by change, perhaps not even made): "You haven't touched the piano / for years, for years I believed / you'd give my words music." Still, change prevents dull sameness; it renews: "You, going gray / have grown new, you've touched me / to lean to see how you feel." Finally, it is change which, while erasing us, permits a carefully modified hope, the future's promise: "As I go / to fell oak I can hear your hands / gaining their way back up the piano." In "Before Sleep" the poet, walking through town before bedtime, aware of his own coming sleep and that of his dead ancestors, holds for a moment before climbing home: "I wait for myself to quiet, breathing / the breath of sleepers I cannot help love." The doubleness of this final phrase knows what can be and what can not: I "cannot help" but love them (the living sleepers and the dead); I "cannot help" them to love. The last poem in *Before Sleep*, "The House in the Trees," describes the construct every artist seeks (the house that "conforms to the hillside," that, "on the verge of being lived in," "receives light / as a guest"), the construct he seeks in the paradoxically limited "freedom of knowing / before it could ever be done / he would have, finally, to leave it." For Booth, this is man's condition, his terror and his hope.

A few poems in *Before Sleep* fail from being too blunt, from replacing creation with statement, from a touch of the maudlin, or from seeming more forced than necessary. However, like "The House in the Trees," most of them are, in meaning and skill, another forward (and "sideways") tack in Booth's continuing and cyclical voyage from knowing we live on "insufficient evidence" to achieving an "awkward . . . faith."

A Final Word

Philip Booth's connection to New England is so obvious as to need little comment. Much of his subject matter, most of his settings, his language, his rhythms, and his tone are taken from his native place. Both his themes and his metaphoric method of relation and revelation are surely centered in the post-transcendental effort of poets like Dickinson, Stevens, and Frost to explore the often paradoxical possibilities and limits of human knowing and making, life and work, and to do so through man's connection and lack thereof with nature. Booth's relation to contemporary poetry is more problematical. His earliest work has clear connections with academic demands for the well-made, closed, iconographic poem. Yet even in those poems, he is rarely allusive, metaphysically difficult, or impersonal, and he is often didactic. Furthermore, he soon progressed—with the general thrust of contemporary verse— toward organic rhythms and autobiographical material. Later, he gave increased attention to such non-rational states as those of memory and dream, shifted his poems away from the finality of closure toward the open-ended, and, eventually, added open forms to closed ones. However, even as he did and does so, Booth maintains the revising control by mind of the poetic process, and he never surrenders that ironic, inclusive sense of the doubleness of things so central to the academic style—not, of course, because it is central to that, but because it is essential to his sense of how things are. At any rate, it is probably best to say that in using aspects of many contemporary modes Booth remains an independent, going his way on his own. His poems, as he said once of Frost's, are "a constant symbol of his life's commitment to making metaphors that clarify the dark paradoxes they contain,"[16] that discover deepening ways of "facing the deep" and the dark.

Chapter Four

"Walking the Boundaries":
The Poems of Peter Davison

Biographical Sketch[1]

Peter Davison was born 27 June 1928, in New York City, son of Natalie Weiner Davison and the Anglo-American poet Edward Davison, Professor of English at the University of Colorado and Director of the Writers Conference in the Rocky Mountains. Davison grew up in Boulder and attended the Fountain Valley School in Colorado Springs, where he was active in athletics, musical theater, and drama, and graduated first in his class. During the last years of World War II, Davison's father did war work in Washington, D.C., and Davison spent his summers there, serving as a page in the U.S. Senate in the summer of 1944.

From 1945 to 1949 Davison was an undergraduate at Harvard College, where he continued his acting and was a member of the Harvard Glee Club and the Signet Society. He graduated *magna cum laude*, with a concentration in History and Literature, and was elected to Phi Beta Kappa. In 1949 and 1950 he did graduate work as a Fulbright Scholar at Saint John's College, Cambridge University. On his return to America he was hired as a "first reader," an apprentice editorial position, by Harcourt, Brace & Company in New York, but six months later was called to military service during the Korean War. From 1951 to 1953 Davison was posted to several American bases as a member of the Second Loudspeaker and Leaflet Company, Psychological Warfare Division, United States Army; he was promoted to the rank of sergeant. After his discharge, Davison returned to New York and Harcourt, Brace, becoming an assistant editor. He remained there until June 1955, when he moved to Cambridge, Massachusetts, where for a year he was Assistant to the Director of Harvard University Press. From this time until 1959 he was also involved in the Poets' Theatre in Cambridge, appearing in, among other plays, the first production of Richard Wilbur's translation of Moliere's *The Misanthrope* and John Ashbery's *The Compromise*. In 1956 Davison became Assistant Editor at the Atlantic Monthly Press. He was promoted to Executive Editor in 1959, began a thirteen-year period as a regular poetry reviewer for the *Atlantic Monthly*, published his first poem ("The Winner"), and married Jane Auchincloss Truslow, herself the author of two non-fiction books, *The Fall of a Doll's House* (1980), a mixture of social, architectural, and personal history, exploring the American dream of the single-family suburban home, and *This Old House* (1981). They have two children.

Peter Davison's first book, *The Breaking of the Day*, won the Yale Series of Younger Poets Award for 1963 and was published in 1964. Also in 1964 he became Director of the Atlantic Monthly Press (a position he held until 1979). His second book, *The City and the Island*, was published in 1966 by Atheneum, which has continued to publish his poems since then. Davison was a member of the board of the National Translation Center from 1967 to 1970, and in 1968 he purchased a house in West Gloucester, Massachusetts, which, with its environs, plays an important role in his later poetry. From then until 1979 he divided his years between summers in Gloucester and winters in Cambridge and, later, in Boston. Also in 1968 Davison became a member of the Atlantic Monthly Company's Board of Directors; he remained on the board until 1980. In 1970 he published his third book, *Pretending to Be Asleep*, and, in 1971, Halty Ferguson of Cambridge issued Davison's elegiac poem for his father, *Dark Houses*, in a handsome limited edition of 300 copies.

In 1971–72 Davison spent a "sabbatical year" in Rome, writing the autobiographical prose of *Half Remembered* and working on the new poems of *Walking the Boundaries*. In 1972 (after a year's hiatus) he resumed the directorship of the Atlantic Monthly Press, began his continuing position as poetry editor of the *Atlantic Monthly*, and received a National Institute of Arts and Letters / American Academy of Arts and Letters Award. In 1972 he published *Half Remembered: A Personal History*, which tells the two-sided story of Davison's first forty or so years. On the one hand it is a story of rich gifts and good fortune: a poet-father, a vibrant Jewish mother, contact from his earliest years with authors—among them J. B. Priestley, Robert Penn Warren, and Robert Frost, an education at Harvard and Cambridge, a successful and rewarding career in publishing, a happy marriage, and the West Gloucester farm. On the other hand it is a story—as one reviewer described it—of gifts and good fortune gained at great costs: "repeated periods of profound depression leading . . . to years of psychoanalysis, indecision concerning his vocation, the frustration of years (most of his twenties) when he was unable to write, an inability to love which led to a string of shallow or tormented relationships. Most of the costs stemmed, it seems, from the turbulent emotional life of his parents . . . who . . . filled his growing life for far more years than is usual and to the exclusion of other persons, including himself."[2] By the end of the years the autobiography covers, Davison had reconciled his gifts and misgivings; he now has his own family, has come to terms with his past, and has found his home and his dual career as editor and poet. Nevertheless, the book ends not complacently, but with an earned self ready to continue facing the hard questions and complex facts of the "crabbed present" of life, of work, and of art.

In 1974 Davison published *Walking the Boundaries: Poems 1957–1974*; in 1977 his fifth collection, *A Voice in the Mountain* appeared. He edited and wrote a preface for *Hello Darkness: The Collected Poems of L. E. Sissman*, published in 1978 and winner of the National Book Critics' Circle Award in Poetry for 1979. Also in 1978 Davison became a member of the Corporation of Yaddo, the artists colony in Saratoga Springs, New York. In 1979 he moved with his family to the Gloucester house full time and, later that year, became Senior Editor of the Atlantic Monthly Press. *The World of Farley Mowat*, a selection from the works of the well-known Canadian ethnologist, nature writer, and historian, edited with a preface by Davison, appeared in the fall of 1980. He has written many, and continues to write, essays and reviews. A new book of poems, *Barn Fever*, was published in 1981.

Theme, Technique, and Development

Peter Davison writes a poetry of the self in search of the self both in its particular and personal and in its larger human contexts. The methods of that search are various, but typically include penetrating, often painful acts of self-examination, and often equally painful explorations of ancestry and of the self's inheritance therefrom. Also typically included is rigorous attention to what make such examination and exploration possible: memory and imagination, both of which can make the self available by keeping or re-creating what is otherwise lost through time, change, and death; both of which also threaten because of their potential for subjective, sometimes evasive, falsification. Davison's search for insight also frequently involves the self's relation to others outside the family, particularly lovers, and—especially in the later poems—to its physical as well as psychic and human environments. He writes, then, a poetry of knowledge, of the attempts, failures, and successes of the self in moving from not knowing to knowing, from knowing falsely to knowing truly, from partial knowing to knowing more complete. The way to this knowledge is always more and more inclusive seeing, a more and more fully tensioned balance between such opposites as inner and outer self, self and other, self and world, chaos and order, fact and idea, life and art. Such a poetry, of course, can never be finished. Even as it closes it must open outward and inward again. Even its achievements of acceptance are necessarily less than complete. For these and other reasons, knowledge is not the end of these poems. They want not only to identify, describe, and define, to know what, but also to know how—how to use what is known of the self to remake the self, how to live.

These remarks perhaps exaggerate the "self-centeredness" of Davison's work, for, to repeat, his poetry also desires to know the world: to know it as the matrix the self inhabits and therefore part of the self's identification, description, and definition, that is, its natural history; to know it as the place in which, in terms of which, the self must learn to act, learn how to act. This doubleness, and its development, is in some measure indicated by the shift in the earlier to the later poetry from a tone frequently of desperation to one of continuing struggle but also of acceptance, and from a largely psychological poetry to what might be called a poetry of landscape. In addition to these essential themes, there is one other—one tied to the moral imperative implicit in the poetry's concern with creating the self, with how to live: Davison's frequent identification, definition, description, and judgment of contemporary manners and mores.

Davison's first book appeared in 1964, more or less precisely as the formalism of the academic establishment was being supplanted by the openings of subject and form effected by the Beat and Confessional breakthroughs of the late 1950s and early 1960s. However, although his own poetry is fundamentally autobiographical and profoundly concerned with the relation of poetry to life ("Poetry was my way of keeping alive"),[3] Davison disliked the excesses of "breast-baring, bottle-draining"[4] confessionalism and, especially, the eschewals of formal and technical control in much of the lesser poetry in these fashionable modes, as his *Atlantic Monthly* reviews of the period show. His own poetry is typically controlled in its revelations and traditional in technique. It is often, though far from always, rhymed, metered (usually in iambics), and in regular stanzas (very occasionally a sestina, a villanelle, or sonnet, frequent quatrains, but more typically nonce forms in regular or irregular stanzas patterned to emphasize structure). It is often marked by the ironic inclusiveness typical of the academic style and is frequently literary (although rarely arcane) in its allusiveness to other writers and to myth. On the other hand, except for occasional clottedness in some earlier poems, Davison's diction is typically plain, unadorned, and natural, the language of ordinary speech used with more than ordinary care and precision and with special attention to the reverberant possibilities and nuances of etymology, connotation, and sound. He also makes much use of narrative structures. Thus, his poems are generally accessible. In his own particular mix, then, Davison combines aspects of the academic mode, of earlier poetries, and of the several types reacting against academic orthodoxy.

Aside from intensifications of skill, most of the technical matters described above remain relatively consistent throughout Davison's career. The more recent poems do show some significant formal loosening and much less rhyme; many of them are in free verse, still more employ versions of blank verse perhaps best described in terms of Frost's categories of tight and loose iambics. However, the major development of Davison's work is not so much a matter of theme or technique as of medium: he has turned increasingly to a narrative-meditative poetry of place and the natural world, especially since the new poems of *Walking the Boundaries*. At any rate, Davison has created in both "media" an important body of poetry that, as Daniel Hoffman described it, is at once "formal and contemporary in feeling."[5]

The Breaking of the Day

Peter Davison's first book, *The Breaking of the Day* (1964), was awarded publication in the Yale Series of Younger Poets. When it appeared, with a foreword by Dudley Fitts, Davison was thirty-six. Behind him, although not left behind, was a long struggle with his own identity and with the inspiring and repressing example of his poet-father. The book collects the poems he had written since that evening in August 1957, when at age twenty-nine, with no writing yet done, he "experienced" his first poem, generated by his reading of the manuscript of Stanley Kunitz's *Selected Poems,* then being prepared for publication by the Atlantic Monthly Press.[6] In the ensuing months and years he worked at his craft, "began gradually to hear [his] own voice as a poet," recognized the centrality of poetry to his life, and "With the growth of confidence that [he] could distinguish [his] poetic imagination and [his] fantasy life, ... began to write poems that dealt directly [although not confessionally] with personal experience."[7]

The Breaking of the Day includes thirty-three such poems, two of them multipart sequences, the whole divided into four sections. They are concerned with the poet's relationships with his parents, and with his own identity—especially as known through those relationships and others, with psychological states, with contemporary manners and mores, with loss—especially death, and with the power or lack of power of memory and imagination to rescue or redeem loss. The techniques used are those of an accomplished, sometimes brilliant, but sometimes too self-conscious craftsman. The language is careful and colloquial, neither elevated nor flat; rhyme is common; meters and stanza forms are more or less regular. There is a good deal of irony, ambivalence, and ideational and emotional point and counterpoint. The autobiographical material is direct and candid but sufficiently distanced and balanced usually to avoid the "chaos of egotistical reflections."[8]

The first nine poems of *The Breaking of the Day* are gathered under the heading "Spells in Sawyer's Cove." The opening one, "Fogged In," announces the theme of loss that unites them all. The first three of its four rhyming iambic trimeter quatrains describe the fog's approach, the fourth, its effect, the loss of contact, of sight and sounds, and—as the poem's metaphor takes hold—of life itself. The "fog has won"

> And blurs us deaf and blind.
> Enshrouded beyond call
> We tremble for the end
> Of islands, echoes, all.[9]

In the blank verse stanzas of " 'True Feeling Leaves No Memory' " (the title is borrowed from Stendhal) Davison records the more particular, although still generalized, loss of a lover, a loss in part depicted by the metaphor of clear-cutting a symbolic landscape. He especially mourns the inability of memory to keep present more than a trace of the lover's presence: "Memory leaves no more than a flash / Of full moon glinting on unfrozen river," saves only a sensual surface. Nevertheless, imagination can create a place to evoke the one where the self "must once have lain," although, as "must" suggests, even this may be mere assumption. Such counterpointed double views are characteristic of *The Breaking of the Day*.

The theme of loss continues in the intricately imagined "North Shore," a two-part poem in something like blank verse sonnets, the parts connected by the metrical completion of the last line of part one by the first line of part two. With its impersonal voice and its title references to the island home of the goddess Aphrodite and the famous pastoral landscape by Watteau, the first section, "The Embarkation for Cytherea," seems at first a straightforward celebration of the sensual pleasures of Brahmin youth, but there are counternotes that lend the poem an air of parody: the young men "Trample the shaven lawn"; the girls are in "platoons," bright and virgin, and their limbs are cool. However, at the moment we perceive and judge the hard unfeeling these counternotes suggest, the poem proceeds to consider the matter from still another vantage. Its second part, "The Return," is spoken, now many years in the future, by one left behind. The brittle sensuality of the young seems life itself against the empty ache of this one's loss:

> Shutters keep out the sun, chairs lie in shrouds,
> The Chinese vases rattle with dry leaves.
>
> . . . .
>
> At night the house is silent, and the wind
> Steals out each dawn to comb a barren sea.

(7)

Related ambiguities fuel "At the Site of Last Night's Fire" where the destructive dangers of intense experience and feeling, perhaps of passion, are compared and contrasted to the cold comfort of memory's healing ash. The major poem of the book's first section is "Not Forgotten," Davison's five-part elegy for his mother, who died a painful death from cancer in September 1959. It benefits greatly from its specificity and directness as it modulates from anguish to reconciliation. Part one, "Watching Her Go," is a frank, sometimes flat description of the mother's death, of her and the watching family's suffering: "The eyes opened. Pain burst at me / As from a cannon's muzzle." The poem ends with an ambiguous image that suggests final acceptance and grace but also the subtle finalities of disappearance and the reduction of self to ragged, falling flesh: "Flaccid, fumbling / At the unravelled edge of herself, / She died like an otter sliding into a pond." The metrical jarrings reflect the emotional welter. Part two, "Dream," records the son's symbolic nightmare of inability to come to terms with his mother's death. Required to pronounce the funeral oration, he cannot speak, cannot remember who is dead, has lost his "Oxford Book of Consolations." Out of this numbness, he acts, madly, movingly:

> So with nothing at all to say, I did what I did:
> Danced a very respectful dance on the coffin.
> The guest of honor drummed her cold toes
> On the underside of the lid.
>
> (10)

The continuing and limited contact this strangely appropriate dance permits is a brilliant image of celebratory, if mute, acceptance. But only in dream. Part three, "Reality," reminds that loss still overwhelms. Contrasting his pain as a nurtured son with those of nurtured friends, he reveals that his anguished dislocation is neither formalized nor stilled: "they turn away with a sigh: they cannot howl / Simply because they are not frightened enough. / They have lost a landmark, not a birthplace."

In "Reality" the metrical irregularities of "Watching Her Go" and "Dream" move toward an iambic norm. In part four, "Self-Defense," that norm is reached. Its iambic trimeter quatrains are ritualistically formal, and the distance the speaker has gained from his experience is further evidenced by his controlled depiction of the shared mix of strength and weakness in his mother and himself. This ritual of recognition releases the reconciled acceptance of the final poem of "Not Forgotten," "Aftermath." The meter is again informal (formality is here, of course, itself a kind of defense), but now it is more relaxed than irregular. For the first time the mother is directly addressed, "you" replacing "her" and "she." The pain persists; in her absence the world is less, but she persists as well: "the bloom of your presence / Is absurd as unicorns / Or buttercups at Christmas." Now the memory that would not function in "Dream" finds her "hovering / In a hundred places," and the poem (having progressed from speechless dance to howl to formal, then graceful, personal speech) can end with a prayer that expresses continuing anguish and fear of loss but also affirms connection and continuing presence: "I pray you do not stray / Farther from us." In this book Davison's most achieved voice is an elegiac one.

The second section of *The Breaking of the Day* again takes its title from one of its poems. "Words for a Slow Movement" collects eleven pieces more or less united by their attention to psychological states associated with sexuality, and by their attention to the contrasts and connections between life's complexities and the perfections (often simplifications) of art and other idealizations, between fact and idea, flesh and mind. The opening piece, the section's title poem, presents a series of perfect surfaces in formal stanzas and indicates the equally attractive, equally essential mysteries beneath them. Its final image is of Botticelli's depiction of the birth of Venus, emphasizing that: under the "naked brightness" of the "shell-borne goddess / Surges ever the restless inscrutable sea." Its ambivalent moral is clear: "Gravity sings beneath the graces of beauty." Several poems about youthful sex lead to the judgmental view in "Summer School" that "These scholars, sworn to seek the limits of self, / Enlarge their own by feeding upon others." These exposures of the gaps between experience and education, between the way things are in fact and the way they are in books, prepare for poems on the limits and powers of art to deal with life. "The Peeper" is the dramatic monologue of a voyeur (another sexual failure) whose prying loving at a distance ("I love at eye's length") is at once moving and perverse, a desperate form of contact and false escape from the dissonant facts of the real. Seen from a certain angle, his predicament mirrors that of the artist who must pry with cold excitement into other lives for material and who always runs the danger of falsifying life by distancing it, purifying it, putting it "under glass." The rhymed couplets of "Sacrificial Mask" consider a similar problem, the cost at which the artist in every self creates a public mask to conceal—and therefore painfully distort—the private self beneath. "Foot" treats the fine balance between freedom and control required for graceful articulation, the metrical pun of its anatomical title enlarging the poem to a note on poetics. A broader and more explicit poetics is stated in "Peripheral Vision," which insists that the poet must find and make "shape and style" but not so fully organize reality as "To tidy up the view / And clear it out of true." Thus, this poem generalizes what the ambiguities of many of these poems had implied. The section ends appropriately with a tribute to Robert Frost's ability to know and express the differences between mind and flesh, real and ideal, art and life, man and matter without falsifying either, a tribute to his containing balance of believing skepticism and skeptical belief.

As its title implies, *The Breaking of the Day*'s third section, "To a Mad Friend," concentrates on extreme psychological states. The title piece introduces the section's twelve poems with the at once distressing and comforting assertion that everyone, no matter how superficially "normal," shares the desperations of the mad. "Finale: Presto" is a fine blank verse dramatic monologue spoken, in this case internally, by a version of the poet's dying mother. (Its connections with "Not Forgotten" are emphasized in the selected poems of *Walking the Boundaries*, where it is printed just before it.) At first, the woman rages at her coming death, her speechlessness, her husband's and her own children's failures to attend and apprehend her as she needs. However, as frustration intensifies, her very anger gives her a courage she had lacked. She overcomes her fear of pain, her loneliness, and her escapist "visions of good order in a future / Near enough to reach for," and is suddenly freed to confront the fact of death, to speak its name, if only to herself. Her feelings are extreme, on some border of madness and ecstasy, but they bring her, if not relief, release:

> "Death." I sing the lovely word again,
> And footsteps start to chatter down the hall
> Towards my bed. Smiling at every sound,
> I see that no one can arrive in time,
> And I, emptying like water from a jug,
> Will be poured out before a hand can right me.
> That word raised echoes of a halleluia.
> Death, do you hear me singing in your key?
>
> (39)

Following some portraits of psychic illness, "After a Nightmare" records a psychoanalytic progress from the immobilizing sickness caused by the repression of undeniable aspects of the self toward the active health enabled by their recognition and their placement within the context of the entire personality. That such health is not easily achieved is made clear in a related poem, "The Winner," in which the super-ego successfully and destructively represses other sides of the psyche. "The Death of the Virgin," after a painting by Rembrandt but clearly autobiographical, recalls an equally destructive psychological inability, in effect a refusal, to perceive the facts of comfort as well as grief. "Artemis" revises the myth of the chaste goddess to create an image of sexuality repressed into destructive madness, *eros* become *thanatos*. The violence of such rigid containment is mirrored in the poem's concentrated imagery, closed verse form, and insistent meter.[10] The last poem of "To a Mad Friend" concerns more public madness. Yoking Herod's slaughter of the innocents to the contemporary threat of nuclear holocaust by the ages' shared preference for the easy decisions of bureaucratic "necessity" over the difficulties of real judgment, "The Massacre of the Innocents: Fragments of Uneasy Conversations" records precisely what the subtitle describes.

The facts of Davison's psychoanalysis, his troubled relations with his parents, his inability to write, and his often distressful love affairs surely underlie the poems of "To a Mad Friend." But in those poems, as in some in earlier sections, the personal is made impersonal, is distanced and objectified. In the last and title section, however, the use of personal material is more direct, as it was in "Not Forgotten." "The Breaking of the Day" is a seven-part sequence that records the poet's efforts to come to terms with the dual ancestry of his impoverished, Anglican, English father and his wealthy, New York, Jewish mother. It partially shares the progress from anguish to qualified acceptance of "Not Forgotten," but is a less successful poem, largely because its emotions seem excessive for its facts, as several reviewers pointed out. This judgment applies, of course, to the poem and not to the experiencing man behind it; it is valid in spite of the fact that the poem's excesses in some ways properly extend the psychological poems of "To a Mad Friend." In any case, the sequence takes its title and some of its material from the Genesis story of Jacob's wrestling with the angel till the breaking of the day to win a sign from God. Davison's wrestling is an introspective one, a struggle with himself, with the facts of his inheritance, with questions of belief, and with his hopes as a writer. The sign he seeks is knowledge of who and what he is.

Part one, "July," expresses extreme anguish: the self is a blistering desert to the self, an anguish barely qualified by an itself qualified prayer. Nevertheless, suffering does seem finally to have led at least to confrontation. "The Birthright" begins that confrontation, recalling the poet's discovery, at thirteen, of his mixed ethnic and religious parentage, and further recalling his parents' subsequent refusal to explain its concealment, to answer his resultant questions, or even to take them seriously. "The Wrestler" records initiation into a sense of sin and an accompanying sense of a need for God—here in part "confused" with the physical father, and an awakening impulse to write, stymied by the lack of a wholly sufficient language (see *Half Remembered,* 146–47). Part four, "The Gift of Tongues," concerns Davison's poet-father's great verbal gifts—later recognized as mostly borrowed and squandered —the gifts he passed on to his son, who slowly came to use them, although in the process he had to experience the distressing but releasing fall of his father from a god to an ordinary man. "The Salt Land" and "The Dead Sea" return to the speaker's mixed religious and ethnic backgrounds. Unable to believe in the Christianity of his upbringing and cut off from his Judaic background by the deaths of his non-religious mother and maternal grandmother, the poet is lost, "no more Christian, no more Jew." Thus, the last line of part six repeats the first line of part one: "The afternoon is dark and not with rain." What the poet's rigorous search of the past has earned is not, as part seven, "Delphi," puts it, "a blessing or a name / But only knowledge," the knowledge that the undirected anxiety of "July" has its source in the absence of identity. Whether such knowledge will lead to identity, to a healing of self, remains unknown, but the sequence ends with a heavily qualified yet achieved assertion that turns the dark last lines of part one ("I lift my hands to half a god / And stammer out a portion of a prayer") slightly toward acceptance and a kind of minor affirmation: "I shall never know myself / Enough to know what things I half believe / And, half believing, only half deny." These themes are not always fully realized here, but they will continue to haunt and inspire Davison's poems. The difficult recognitions earned in their introspective wrestlings serve him well in later work.

The Breaking of the Day is, then, an impressive first book. In spite of several weak poems, it establishes many of Davison's major themes, demonstrates a broad range of technical skills, and contains many excellent poems (especially "North Shore," "At the Site of Last Night's Fire," "Not Forgotten," "Winter Sunrise," "Finale: Presto," and "Artemis"). However, the rich promise of

The Breaking of the Day is only partly fulfilled in Davison's next collection two years later in 1966.

The City and the Island

This work, *The City and the Island*, is rather less organized (and less narrow) than indicated by its categorical section headings: "The City and the Island," "The City," and "The Island." However, there is a general, if easily overstated, sense in which the categories do suggest the unified or relatively distinct treatment of such opposing pairs as public and private, external and internal, experience and imagination, and real and ideal. Nevertheless, it is probably more precise to say that Davison uses the volume's many *symbolic* landscapes to continue his exploration of such matters as identity, extreme and "normal" psychological states, contemporary mores, and the relationship of art to life: all of them loosely joined, as before, by a central awareness of the dangers of purifying and falsifying extremes and of the need for inclusive, balanced wholeness in life and in art.

The City and the Island still makes much use of autobiographical material, but that use is less frequently direct and more thoroughly impersonal than in *The Breaking of the Day*. The concern with craftsmanship continues. There is a good deal of blank verse; several poems in rhymed and unrhymed quatrains; another in something like heroic couplets; some with intricate, if irregular, rhyme schemes; one villanelle. The use of regular and shaped stanzas to indicate structure and development remains typical. The diction is still direct and declarative, although, more often than before, as David Galler points out in his review, "the language at times seems insufficient to the psychological complexities it is asked to carry."[11] The counterpointing inclusion of opposing ideas and feelings remains the method by which the poems progress.

The first and title section of *The City and the Island* contains nine poems joined by varied uses of the antipodal landscapes the title identifies. The best and clearest of these is "The Emigration," where the city-island theme is expanded to include the concern with ancestry so essential to *The Breaking of the Day*. The speaker explains to his lover his reasons for shuttling from city to island and back again: in order to live successfully in the mature, external, public but also potentially superficial and concealing world represented by the city, he must confront the inner, private, psychological, threatening but revealing world of islands, must confront his id and ego selves and his parental and personal pasts, recognize who and what he is and that there is no escaping these worlds and these selves. The journey is never complete, but as the refrain-like repetition suggests ("Halfway between the city and the island I / Am bound for the city"), its direction and goal are established and constant. The goal is achievement of the unified, aware, accepting but developing self of psychological health, a self capable of living in the complex world of others.

The thirteen poems of the second section of *The City and the Island*, "The City," are more direct explorations of public and private selves. "They That Have Power to Hurt" takes its title and its concern with the distinction between potential action and chosen deed from Shakespeare's Sonnet 94 ("They that have power to hurt and will do none"). It invokes the conventional idea that man is an essentially tool-making, tool-using animal ("Mankind / Was never itself until / It learned to take tools to task") to further suggest that the evasive rationalization, the transfer of blame, that the quotation also describes is itself essentially human. The poem proceeds to insist that—whatever our tools—the power to hurt is our own, and so, too, the responsibility and guilt resulting from its use. Subsequent poems vary in tone, but by far the best of them is "Easter Island: The Statues Speak," where idea, fact, and voice are brought together in a convincing whole as the psychological themes of the volume coalesce. Standing for the personal and public mysteries of the psyche and of the past that man insists on digging into and digging up, the statues speak of their irritation at being uncovered and of the necessity, the efficacy, the futility, and the danger of such internal and external acts of exploration, discovery, and knowledge. That complex of gains and losses, satisfactions and dangers is the complex of man's condition:

Our feet stood fathoms underground. Thin soil
Clothed us to our chins. How we hoped
To be forgotten! Now these new arrivals,
Who place unearthly burdens on God, unearth us.
They prop us upright for the hundredth time.
They will gladly let us sleep again
Once they have learned the reasons for our silence.

(29)

The final section of *The City and the Island*, "The Island," has fifteen poems, less thematically centered but more often successful than those of the opening and middle sections. The first several poems are connected by "monstrousness." "Eurydice in Darkness" is exemplary. Spoken by Eurydice herself, it re-imagines the Orpheus myth in order to convert her from the traditional willing lover (hoping for rescue but failed by her artist-lover) to a teasing harpy who prefers the underworld and who toys cruelly with the struggling, somewhat silly poet-singer. This makes a fine story in its own right; it may also be the successfully objectified treatment of a failed love affair. Several other pieces also note again the self-destruction inherent in extremes of mind or flesh.

The themes of the remaining poems of "The Island" are more varied, although they are loosely connected by considerations of life and art, spirit and flesh. The relationship of art to life, its limits and possibilities, is the subject of "Of the Painting of Portraits There is No End." In balanced eight-line stanzas spoken by a portrait artist, it describes first his female subject (who attempts to conceal her sensual, physical self in a decorative, formal pose: "Her hands lie smoldering in her lap"), and then the painter himself, who, because he must have order and represent surface, must hope to catch the external echoes of internal reality if his art is not to conceal but "rescue" and reveal. "Epitaph for S. P." involves the dangerous intersections of art and life in the case of the poet Sylvia Plath, with whom Davison had a brief and rather strained affair in 1955.[12] It describes her in terms of a candle badly cast and burning either hardly at all or so intensely as to burn itself out. The poem is especially effective in its shape and in its abruptly shortened final line. It should be read in conjunction with his own later "The Heroine."

One of the best poems of *The City and the Island* is "Winter Fear." Akin to "Winter Sunrise" in *The Breaking of the Day* in its use of a mode here atypical but later central to Davison's work, "Winter Fear" is a Frostian meditation on the seasons, on loss and resistance, and on cyclical permanence and change. Its ambiguities of fact and chastened hope are skillfully handled: "The weather tells of famine and defeat, / Of lying leaves and how we were betrayed / By spring. But winter never yet has won." Another fine poem is the beautifully phrased "Having Saints," which expresses the human need for, in addition to an ultimately mysterious God, minor deities sufficiently anthropomorphic for us to understand and, in turn, to understand us.

Perhaps the best poem of *The City and the Island*, however, is its next-to-last, "Gifts," which treats the dangers of wishing and the paradoxical nature of wishes granted, of gifts, including inspiration. The poem can speak for itself.

> When I was a child, a heartstruck neighbor died
> On her birthday. Dying was strange enough,
> But what a way to choose to spend your birthday,
> I thought, and what sort of a gift was this?
> From time to time, people have done it since—
> Dying in the environs of a celebration
> As though they had picked out the day themselves.
> Perhaps they had, one way or another,
> Prayed for something to happen, and prayed wrong.
> .   .   .   .
> I keep a wary silence on my birthdays,
> Make up no lists at Christmas, lie low
> When asked what I *really* want. How should I know?
> Best ask for gifts as though I had none coming.

(53)

"Passages for Puritans" closes the book, exposing in five sections
the destructive dangers of seeing life in part rather than whole. It
appropriately repeats the volume's unifying theme and ends with
a statement of what is now a central belief and a poetic principle,
of the need—in life and art—for inclusiveness and balance, the
need to sing, as the bird does, both of the "sweet / Lift and totter
of sustaining air" and "of the mound of feathers on the hill," to
sing "with feet upon the swaying branch."

In spite of its thematic coherence and skillful craft, *The City
and the Island* is in many ways a rather weak collection, as indi-
cated by its sketchy treatment here. Too many uncited poems are
unclear because incompletely worked out; there are too many
lapses of tone and of aural control; there are bad lines, like these,
from "A Far Countree": "I frequently have words with telephone, /
Quack at it, savor in return, / The quacks that quack for me";
other poems are overcome by banal sentimentality. Nevertheless,
in its best poems, already discussed, *The City and the Island* points
toward things to come. *Pretending to Be Asleep* (1970) is a
better book.

Pretending to Be Asleep

A common theme of *The Breaking of the Day* and *The City
and the Island* insists that full knowledge and acceptance of the
complexity of things is essential to successful life and art. The
effort to perceive and assent to things as they are—the many and
various, often conflicting aspects of the psyche, the beauties and
horrors, losses and legacies of the past, and the mix of good and
evil, order and disorder in the world—is more consciously central
still in both the public and personal poems of Davison's third
book. *Pretending to Be Asleep* also follows its predecessors in its
ways of knowing and accepting, its techniques. In May Swenson's
description it uses "music and measure directly stemming from
traditional poetics."[13] Many of its poems employ rhyme, several in
regular patterns. Quatrains remain a frequent form, and the use of
regular stanzas to mark organization and development persists.

So, too, do ironic and other, more direct ambivalence and occasional more or less accessible literary allusiveness. Still balancing these traditional characteristics, however, is the experimental language of ordinary, unelevated speech, handled so as to be rich as well as plain.

Many of the thirteen poems of the first section of *Pretending to Be Asleep*, "The Pleaders," are rather public in voice and are connected by their recording of failures of or demands for the self to give full attention and recognition not merely to parts but to the whole complex of experience and reality, as the F. M. Cornford epigraph indicates. Even the two more private opening poems share this connection, if less directly than the others. "After Being Away" celebrates the constant presence of a loved one, whether absent or not, but its poet-speaker also insists on qualifications that broaden the poem's inclusiveness. Speaking about himself, he is pleased that he has "managed to record" some of life's illuminating moments, its "surprises," but adds that he "held no certain magic," "threw no light before" him, and only discovered such moments by stumbling on them. Celebrating his relationship to his lover and the connection of that relationship to his work, he also confesses complicating acts of complicity and selfishness:

> Forgive me for inflicting
> my pride on your surprises
> and holding to the few
> that were my sole possession.
> (3)

The insistently rhymed "Making Marks" asserts a personal poetics of individual, individualizing speech sound. It, too, is informed by a sense of inclusiveness, as a brief quotation will show: "Smiling, though soft in cheek, is hard in bone, / And sounds make words by trickling over stone / To give the tongue an edge to call its own."

The less personal voice of the third poem of "The Pleaders," "Castaway," provides a transition to the more public poems to follow. Whether we take it literally or in terms of the psychological metaphor it suggests, "Castaway" places us at sea, "out of sight / of city and island." The sea tempts us to be less than human, to merge with it; it

> withers hands and fingers
> and invites the drying flippers
> to spread like fans, the fins
> to gather into a tail,
> and, smooth as a seal, the trunk
> without so much as a whisper
> to thrum its way to the bottom.
>
> (5)

This, of course, as the poem makes clear, is the loss of self, is death. It is only at the edge between the tugging, tempting opposites of outer and inner, public and private self, of self and other, self and world, of earth and sea, only there where they overlap yet stay distinct, that any one of them has meaning. It is there a man must balance.

The next several poems of the first section are public, some of them direct critiques of current social ills. Its indictment of false simplifications implied by the severed appendage of its title, "The Gun Hand" is a catalog of contemporary violence. The related "Visions and Voices" exposes complex responses and failures of response, by the speaker and the nation, to the life and death of the assassinated Robert Kennedy, whose "image aroused our desire and nudged our hatred." The danger of partial views, a major source of social as well as personal evils, is more explicitly discussed in other poems. The section's title piece, "The Pleaders," is spoken by the collective voice of the used, ignored, and oppressed —in psychological terms the repressed aspects of self, in social terms those whom the elite, the politicians, educators, managers, and bureaucrats, seek to control and direct, supposedly for their own good. But they refuse to be kept or kept down. They plead for freedom, attention, recognition, and inclusion. They insist on their constant presence: *"We are your children, whom you treat like horses. / We are among you; we are going to stay."* Two poems are portraits of their oppressors. The rhymed quatrains and repeated rhyme words of "The Forked Tongue" expose the false inclusiveness of a "double-dealer" who manipulates the "language of guilt" for his own profit. "Plausible Man" depicts the sort of sociological bureaucrat who has no identity, whose views are always public, whose comforting and apparently informed organizational systems actually ignore the most basic and personal of possible facts: "The plans do not allow for such an implausible / outcome as dying in a room alone." Other sorts of falsification by simplification are the themes of "What Counts" and "The Origin of Species."

If these poems criticize failures of inclusion, "A Word in Your Ear on Behalf of Indifference" presents an exemplary act of inclusion. Its insinuating legal voice praises the protective power of indifference to save nations from war, lovers from destructive passionate excess, the self from suicidal introspection. At the same time, it subtly demonstrates the collateral danger of such inattention: poverty and torture ignored, love lukewarm, the unexamined life. Again, it is implied that a difficult balance between claims and counterclaims is the only hope.

The last two poems of "The Pleaders" concern inclusiveness and art. "The Losing Struggle" describes the artist's effort more constantly to perceive the meanings ("the words for life") in the "never interrupted" surfaces of things, in "every moment present / But hardly every moment seen." This effort is attractive, but dangerous, too. It demands isolation and selection, and, therefore, the attempt to see and see into or through specifics, the very acts of attention, can also promote failures of attention ("Here by the sea I cannot see as far as the mountains"). The demand for order can similarly lead to a distorting preference that ignores the facts of change ("I have come to worship the sun, clouds, clarity, / And as deeply I distrust the moon"). Carried to extremes, the noble urges to see and know and shape can separate pattern from purpose, form from function, and make of the artist "an old spider

who does not care for flies / And webs it for the sake of design."
Art thus simplified, isolated, abstracted from life is not art at all,
but—the only and final perfection—death. It "freeze[s] the world
in light," is motionless, "fixed on what exists beyond existence,"
ignoring what exists. Thus the poem examines the problem of
all art, and of life as well: how to include and balance the claims
of specific and general, fact and idea, particular and meaning,
content and form, disorder and order, things as they are and
things as we would have them be. There is no solution, only the
struggle to balance and contain, one that must always be waged,
although it is always—given what we are—a losing one. This is
Davison's most compelling statement of his poetics, and a central
theme, so far. The last poem of this first section, "Afterwards," in
rhyming five-line stanzas, is a similar piece, in which a maker's
voice, like the spider of the previous poem, tempts the reader into
a garden that is, in its false, exclusionary perfection, the web of
death.

Related to the volume's first section by its implied concern with
inclusive seeing, the fourteen poems of the second section, called
"Pretending to Be Asleep," offer a many-sided consideration of the
limits and possibilities of necessary, accidental, and / or willed
states of awareness and unawareness, waking and sleeping, expe-
rience and imagination. This section also considers the relation-
ship of such states to poetic making, sometimes explicitly, as in
the epigraph from Coleridge. For Davison, poetry and life remain
inseparable. The first poem of the sequence presents the poet-
speaker suffering from speechlessness. Deserted by his words, he
pretends they do not matter. Yet the very mask of unconcern he
adopts shows them to be the essence of his life: "I wear the mask
of an actor who returns / From a long journey to find his wife
and children dead." From this feigned unawareness, the second
poem, the sonnet "In the Dock," proceeds to recognition. If day's
wakefulness can conceal the self from the self, the night, in dream
or in imagination, exposes: "My second sight / Fixes me steadily
within its aim / And squeezes slowly." The squeezing is painful,
but, against the wordlessness of part one, it brings release: "I

awake / To hear the sounds I never thought to make." The release is ambivalent; the sounds are desperate, but preferable to silence. However, even this much release is short-lived. In "Under Protection" the self again marshalls its defenses against the world and others, against the impinging threat of its own complex experience. It happily, self-destructively, dreams the repressive super-ego as a dictatorial fascist. It buys neatness at great cost. As the *abcb* quatrains of the fourth poem, "The Flower of Sleep," imply, sleep brings not difficult, releasing recognition, as in "In the Dock," but a self-swallowing comfort more threatening than the peril it hoped to escape. Nevertheless, it is sleep that reveals the danger:

> lately I dream of sleep,
> Of wrecks and falling trees,
> Of flowers laced around my waist
> And grappling at my knees.
>
> (24)

In these and subsequent sections, "Pretending to Be Asleep" shuttles back and forth between voices of despair and hope, of self-awareness as destructive threat and saving comfort, of unawareness as delusive defense and the source of healing imaginative insight. In the ninth part of the sequence, however, the speaker recognizes and acknowledges all of those preceding voices as his own: whoever speaks, "the infant," "the child," "the grown man wheedling / In rut or yearning in prayer," or "the sexless ancient, dreaming of sex," the "voice is me, whatever voice or stream, / The voice of history rising through my sources." This acceptance of the complex aspects of the self and of the persistence of the past in the present releases, as it were, four poems in which the various speakers listed in "The Voices" have their say. They are at once personal and distanced, part of, less, and perhaps more than the self and its past and present. Their movement is now from defensiveness and evasion toward aware maturity and hope. The first is in the child's voice. It records his concealment of his real self from others, in this case, his parents. Reading in bed, he hears their footsteps on the stairs, shuts off his light, pretends to be asleep: "They will not find the scent / Of hate on me tonight." In "Second Voice: The Youth" a youngster is startled awake by an initiatory dream of death. His response is confused, but more than merely evasive:

> Now should I stand to arms
> After such warning,
> Or pace the aisles of night
> Until morning?
>
> (31)

In "Third Voice: The Widower" the speaker is numbed by his loss, but he recognizes his evasiveness and from that recognition comes a qualified hope in a minor key:

> I know the sun by name.
> This darkness may give ground
> If I dream my way awake,
> Pretending to be asleep.
>
> (32)

This is ambiguous, of course. It may be rhetoric or real. For now, there is no way to know. However, although still more potential than fact, the hope in "Fourth Voice: The Grandmother" is more sure. An old woman complains that the young men around her are fully unaware and bemoans her own lost beauty and sexuality, but her concerned desire that the young awaken, the imaginative power of her memories, her implicit belief in the values of human contact and of life, and her dreams dreamed not in selfishness but in hope for others all outweigh her loss. Awareness that is at once imaginative and in touch with fact is at least possible. This is as far as the sequence will go. Its final poem, "Possession," returns to the relationship of unawareness and awareness to the making of poems. As the title's pun on being possessed and owning suggests, both are needed, mysterious inspiration and conscious revision: "Possession they say is nine points in the poem." Thus, in the course of the sequence, although far from smoothly or directly, the speaker has progressed from anguished wordlessness through defensive evasion, recognition, acceptance, and chastened hope, to confidence that—given inspiration—he can "take over," and attend to the real work of wording his self, his experience, and his world. The ambiguities of waking and sleeping remain as open as before ("Pretending to Be Asleep" may be false conceal-ment or imaginative insight), but the speaker now at least has hope that inclusion of and balance between them might sometime be achieved.

As the first and second sections of *Pretending to Be Asleep* are relatively public and private respectively, the third section consists of personal material sufficiently distanced to be made public. All its poems are more or less directly autobiographical, and—as suggested by the title, "The Years," and by the Thomas Hardy epigraph from which it is taken ("Ah, No. The years, the years. / Down their carved names the raindrop ploughs")—most of them involve attempts both to recall and accept the familial and personal past. The first, "Old Photograph," again expresses the poet's complex response to his mother's death. One of Davison's best poems, it should be read with "Not Forgotten," "Finale: Presto," and "The Death of the Virgin" from *The Breaking of the Day.* Carefully dated to the day after the anniversary of his mother's death, her birthday, the poem is spoken eight years after the event. In it, the speaker records what his continuing pain at once proves and belies, that "No trace" of her is left to him but a few fading photographs and letters. His troubled effort to retrieve or at least recall her is perfectly imaged: "The needle of memory scratches / In the effort to remember," but according to him all that remains is her "propped-up pose . . . / Rigid on the mantle in pious memory." Nevertheless, real memory does come back. He recalls his sharing of his mother's pain, her struggling speechless death, and, then, the comfort offered him by others: the promise that he would soon forget the agonizing parts of her life and death and retain only attractive memories of her. This— at the very moment he records such memories, her "husky laughter," her "charm in company," the "glee" she "took in never / Saying goodby on the telephone"—he insists is false, that all he can remember of her is "grief, sleeplessness, / Infant despair, betrayal." Such insistence, of course, is as false as the promise itself, and the fact that these remarks are prefaced by the quotation from Stendhal that Davison has used before, "True feeling / Leaves no memory," should suggest another avenue of hope. Even if he can only remember pain, the aphorism might show that memory the false one and prove that, since it has left "no memory," "true feeling" did indeed exist. However, he rejects this comfort, too. By the end of the poem it is clear that his inability or refusal to remember his mother as the complex person she was, his insistence on having only the good or the bad, has frozen him into a pose as propped-up as hers on the mantle, as "frozen, as rigid, as blind." There is insight here, self-recognition, and continuing effort, but, at least for now, it releases no contact, "How can I keep in touch / When there is nothing to touch?" The idea that inclusive seeing is essential to successful living continues to underlie the poems of *Pretending to Be Asleep* and the speaker's relative failure to achieve such seeing in "Old Photograph" leaves him immobile and lost. In the next several poems he is more successful.

For instance, the five-part sequence "Words for My Father," has many parallels to the recognitions of "The Breaking of the Day." Although somewhat unbalanced by its excessive comparison of the poet and his parents to Telemachus and Odysseus and Penelope, and, later, of the poet to Odysseus and his father to Laertes, the poem travels convincingly from the poet's admiration of his father and of his verbal skills to his recognition of his and their limits, to his hope for a reconciliation of father and son in the proffering and acceptance of inheritance, the acknowledgment and proof of self, the gift and gift returned of words.

The penultimate poem of "The Years" section of *Pretending to Be Asleep*, "Calypso," is less personal than those that precede it, although the poet's earlier comparison of himself to Odysseus does suggest autobiographical parallels, perhaps even a distanced self-portrait. At any rate, the blank verse retelling of the Odysseus-

Calypso story, from the goddess's point of view (a revision related to that in the earlier "Eurydice in Darkness") creates a parable of the complex of limited, striving self and of the painful balance of inclusive, accepting seeing. The book concludes with "Stumps," a personal statement of poetics which, like "Winter Sunrise" and "Winter Fear," makes subtle metaphoric use of precise natural description in a way that will be typical of Davison's later work. Like memories of the dead, of the past, the stumps put out new shoots, alive but weak; like the poet who both controls and employs the matter of his past, their owner will neither let them grow uncontrolled nor poison them out. If not the usual one, they are nonetheless a kind of crop, permitting a kind of harvest.

Pretending to Be Asleep is a good book. Thematically coherent, its poems, with few exceptions, are well and clearly realized in their complex ambiguities. Its tonalities are richly controlled, the bad lines and lapses into sentimentality or bathos of *The City and the Island* are largely left behind, and here abstractions are more typically rendered in convincingly appropriate particulars. Some weak poems like "The Gun Hand" and "The Forked Tongue," are outweighed by far more good ones and several of real excellence, among them "After Being Away," "What Counts," "A Word in Your Ear on Behalf of Indifference," "The Losing Struggle," "Old Photograph," "Calypso," and "Stumps." But Davison's major breakthrough comes in his next collection.

Walking the Boundaries: Poems 1957–1974

Davison's fourth book, *Walking the Boundaries*, appeared in 1974. It contains forty-eight selected poems (sixteen from *The Breaking of the Day*, fifteen from *The City and the Island*, seventeen from *Pretending to Be Asleep*) and twenty-five new ones. The selected poems are printed first, rarely and then only slightly alerted from their original appearances. A few titles have been changed, and a few of the sequences altered when only parts of them are reprinted. Errors of punctuation in the original printings have been corrected. However, aside from the selection itself, the major change in the selected poems is in their arrangement. Davison's first three books were typically arranged in sections organized so that poems comment on and qualify one another. Although occasional new relationships are made clear by the present, perhaps more chronological ordering (the juxtaposition, for example, of "Finale: Presto" and "Not Forgotten," or the opening use of "Peripheral Vision" as an announcement of method), much of the sequential effect of the earlier patterns is lost. Even distinctions among the original volumes and between the selected and new poems are indicated only in the table of contents. But these are minor matters. It is the new poems that concern us here.

To a point, the themes of *Walking the Boundaries'* new poems are consistent with those of previous volumes. Davison's effort to know the self through introspection and through examination of the self's relations to the familial and personal past, to parents and lovers, continues, as do poems of psychological extremes, of elegy, of social comment, and on poetics. The belief in the healing potential of inclusive recognition persists. However, in these poems a new subject, nature, a change in milieu from the realm of psychology to landscape, is newly attended to, and a new tone, a new attitude, somehow alters their themes. This is best described as a newly achieved power of balanced but never complacent acceptance, even of affirmation—no doubt stemming in part from the attainment of psychological health and relative personal happiness recorded in the poet's autobiography. Dangers and threats to the self continue and continue to be recognized and confronted, but now they rarely overwhelm, and the desperate shrillness of balance unbalancing that often marked earlier poems is unusual in these.

Technically, the new poems continue to use stanzas as indicators of experiential and poetic structure, but they almost never employ externally determined forms and are rarely rhymed. They are still characterized by ironic and other ambiguities, as well as by some literary allusions and by narrative patterns. Diction remains resolutely and richly plain. Several poems are still in blank verse, but, more generally, Davison persists in using an iambic base around which substitutions are made. There are more substitutions than before, more extreme variations in length of line, and more free verse than in any previous collection. Generally put, the poems maintain a shapeliness of movement, but now the shapeliness is more fully organic than imposed.

The new poems of *Walking the Boundaries* are framed by the four parts of the title work which, taken together, form an extraordinary sequence. Two of them appear in the opening and closing positions, the other two are placed within the body of the collection. They will receive comment as a unit later in this discussion. Following the opening "Walking the Boundaries" poem, the second of the new poems, "Is Anything Wrong?," is a relatively general treatment of one of Davison's continuing themes: the problem of subjectivity, the difficulty of knowing the self ("What sort of creature am I inside of?") and the world ("These lilypads, these ghostly ginkos and herons / stretch up their presences from the anti-world"). It ends in a containing mix of mutually qualifying despair and hope:

> Pressing closer to the knowledge
> that there is no knowledge, that our world
> is visions, shadows, I hear it rumored
> that perhaps, who knows, we are living in a cave?
>
> (66)

The desperation of a total subjectivity that makes knowledge impossible is countered by the possibility of our knowing we cannot know, itself a paradoxically objective knowledge capable (as the last line's reference to Plato's parable of the cave suggests) of providing complex illumination. Indeed, instead of closing off possibilities, the problem of knowledge—see that oddly placed final question mark—opens them up.

Difficult questions about the nature of the self persist in *Walking the Boundaries*, but they are typically examined or posed with an aware acceptance of both limitations and possibilities at a distance from the more pained and less controlled extremes of earlier efforts. Nevertheless, this balance does not lead to smugness. Several poems, both personal and impersonal, continue to depict and explore states of psychological disturbance or distress. "Doors" is one of these, an intricate, controlled meditation on the distressing ways in which the self contains the past and, more distressing still, the ways in which the past contains the self. With its portrait of a dementedly intense and violent protective, devouring love, "Poem of Force" is another (compare with "Artemis" and "Eurydice in Darkness"). So, too, is "Bandages," with its concrete depiction of the night's failure to heal the self to face another day. In "Valentines" Davison paints an almost surreal portrait of a man haunted, drained, and suffocated by his past and its commitments. So this poem, too, belongs to this group. Perhaps the best of these poems of psychological extremity, however, is "Bed Time." It opens with the real but ordinary distress of the insomniac: "Few beds are stonier than one shared by a sleeper / and a waker who stares into the dark / listening to the house breathe." It then proceeds brilliantly to capture the intensifying, hallucinatory horrors of the man who hovers between sleep and waking, imagination and memory, dream and fact, who suffers fragmentary haunting by the shared location of past love and future death with nothing to fall back on but that location, his bed.

Other subjects and concerns typical of other volumes are continued here. Both "The Heroine" (again about Sylvia Plath) and the "Obituary Writer" (about John Berryman) exhibit not only Davison's continuing elegiac bent, but also, in their exposures of their author as well as of his subjects, the way in which his thematic concerns typically overlap in his constant effort to know the self more fully. The major poem of this sort in *Walking the Boundaries* is "Dark Houses," Davison's elegy for his father, which will be more appropriately discussed elsewhere. Another poem extending earlier concerns into this volume—this time, abiding love and dissolving time—is the splendid "Ground," which begins with rich description of the changefulness of nurturing earth and then subtly shifts to show the loved one to be her lover's ground, her intimate presence informing him as the earth informs its crops and the sea the defining colors of fish, and—at the same time—to expose his fears of losing her and his sense that to do so would be to lose his essential self—as picked fruits lose flavor, caught fish color. The poem's effects are more delicate, stronger, and more natural than such a paraphrase expresses.

The thematic continuities of *Walking the Boundaries'* new poems with Davison's earlier work are clear in spite of some changes in technique from the previous volume to this one. In fact, the fair amount of metrical loosening in their frequent turn from traditional poetics to free verse seems less revolutionary than a logical and natural extension of Davison's always virtuosic and various handling of meter and line. However, an important development in these poems is a change in attitude or tone, the roots of which are largely to be found in events in Davison's personal life: a change from desperate struggle to continuing but now accepting struggle and of earned and qualified affirmation. The change is neither so simple nor so distinct as such a statement makes it sound. Earlier poems record struggles toward inclusive recognition and acceptance, often as their central themes; and they sometimes achieve affirming reconciliations. The new poems, too, are marked by continuing anguish and loss, by harsh critiques of self and world. However, the still struggling, still searching speaker and maker of the new poems is everywhere in fuller control of himself and his experience than before, more poised in his acts of inclusion, in his admission of the limits of the self, of ancestry, of knowledge, and of time, and he is more successful, even certain, in his attainment of and chastened satisfaction with actual and qualified affirmations. This success is easily exaggerated, but real, and is, of course, a matter of poetic as well as personal advance. Davison now writes poems of inclusion, recognition, and acceptance where he earlier more often wrote abstractly *about* such acts, about the need for them, and this shift is surely as much a matter of more mature method as of more mature personality. At any rate, the slight skewing of the qualifications of "Is Anything Wrong?" toward hope remarked above will serve as an example. A better way to get at these developments, though, is to examine a poem which takes as its subject changes in the self, in philosophy, and in poetics.

"Standing Fast: Fox into Hedgehog" borrows its title and its metaphors from a fragment by the Greek poet Archilochus, "The fox knows many tricks, the hedgehog only one. / One good one,"[14] some of the implications of which have been worked out in Isaiah Berlin's famous essay on Tolstoy, "The Hedgehog and the Fox," where he separates writers into the foxes of diversity and the hedgehogs of unity.[15] Davison's treatment of the various oppositions the contrast suggests is, of course, less abstract, and less clear-cut. The poem describes the metamorphosis of the image of self from that of the youthful, flashy, nearly frenetic fox, whose defenses are elaborate tricks and who gets into everything, into that of the hedgehog, slow, stable, more a settler than a traveler, dull in color, defended not by disguise but by self-containment. It is a humorous poem and measures the losses as well as the gains of such a change, but its final image is of earned control, balance, and real if limited certainty: "I . . . / . . . Stand fast, here, now. / No call to run quick. I know what I know." It is from this rooted, confident (if still besieged: "Quarry for all comers, I crouch in furrows, / keep away from the light, bristle at a footfall") location of self in time and place and knowledge that the new poems of *Walking the Boundaries* are made, and that makes them Davison's finest collection so far, a breakthrough into the characteristic voice of his mature work, the voice that appears in two of the best of these poems, "Dark Houses" and the four-part "Walking the Boundaries."

Davison's father died in early 1970. The son's elegy, "Dark Houses: for Edward Davison (1970–1898)," was first published in a limited edition in 1971 and later included in *Walking the Boundaries*. As the inversion of the dates in its title dedication indicates, the first six of the poem's seven sections tell, backward, through selected moments, the story of the dead poet's life. Part one, "At Seventy-One. New York," opens with fact: "Words have finally failed this balloon of a body, / White as a side of bacon, cold as the plank / It heightens like foothills under a sheet in

the morgue." Nevertheless, it is words, his father's great and
wasted gift, and his gift to his son, their successes and failures,
that unite the poem as clearly as biography does. The son's judg-
ment is at once accurate, harsh, and loving. Alive, poetry had
"smoldered" in his father, awake but somehow smothered, "Like
January wasps that stir in summer houses." He had "squandered"
his words. Nevertheless, "In spite of years and years of wearing
down, / The words whose slave he was could still surprise him."
For good and ill, as ways of getting at truth and as delusive tricks,
"Words, and the songs of words, convinced his life." These acts
of description, admiration, and criticism resolve into the finality
of loss in the final line: "No words go walking in a darkened
house."

The second section, "*At Fifty. Pennsylvania*," describes the
anguish of his father's decline: his troubled sense of betrayals
"given and received," his drinking "like a punishment / To keep his
heart from thumping with the shame / Of memory and waste," his
buried but still haunting hate for the father who deserted him,
his not quite satisfactory replacement of that father with the
praise of older men, and his burial of his other loves in a wife
"who never calmed him but inflamed / His anger." As all of this
suggests, his ghosts would not stay down, but came "bursting out
in coughs that stretched and tore" and "racked him with a
daily taste / Of all that wrestles poetry to earth." In addition
to their finely emphatic portrayal of suffering, these lines also
suggest a complex analysis of the reasons for the elder Davison's
artistic failure. There is the romantic, but at least partially true
idea that the beauty of poetry was destroyed in him by the
brutalities of life. More convincing, however, is the thought that,
although he had the kind of experience that can "wrestle" poetry
down from an inflated, sententious, disconnected empyrean to
the real welter of earth, he was unable to make poetic use of that
experience, unable therefore to make lasting poems. The next
four sections of "Dark Houses" continue this clear-eyed and lov-
ingly inclusive examination and re-creation of his father's life and
his poetic successes and failures.

"At Forty. Colorado" describes his settling in America and his trading of poetry for teaching ("students clustered around"; "poetry is what he spent for them") and identity ("He came into his own as son and father / Just as he, knowingly, went down as poet"). The tone is descriptive and, if judgmental, not accusatory. The loss of poetry happened; "Desertion is not charged in this affair." "At Thirty. On Tour" recalls his wooing and winning of Davison's mother and his real but never trusted successes as a poet, and "At Twenty-Two. Cambridge," his brilliant years at university and the beginning of the long decline and wastage of his talent. "At Sixteen. South Shields" describes his impoverished, fatherless childhood, his youthful enlistment in the Royal Navy and his first bright discovery of another world through reading poetry and in Cranmer's Book of Common Prayer. Part of the poem's real power comes from this writing of the father back, as it were, into life. Along with often potent language, startling honesty (the fullness not of malice but of loving memory), and forgiving understanding (the implied recognition that his father's discovery of poetry as a means of escape made it inevitable that his poetry be escapist), it is this re-writing that wrestles to earth the poetry in the necessary "prosiness" of the poem's biographical fact. The final section of "Dark Houses" returns to the present to describe the casting of the father's ashes from a cliff on his son's land. Sorrow, reconciliation, and a continuing sense of the father's failure inform the piece. So, too, does a promise. In this line, "Surviving him, we carry the poet's flesh" (which in the next line goes on to this: "Reduced to ashes in a canister"), there is more than simple fact. There is also the acceptance of inheritance, large and reduced, and the results of that acceptance, the father's gift returned, this poem.

In addition to the new quality of balanced acceptance already described as the major development of these poems, another important advance in them stems in part from Davison's purchase of the Gloucester salt-water farm that is now his home and in part from his achievement of sufficient psychological balance to allow him what might be called a more objective mode of subjectivity. This advance is a new attention to the natural world as a source of images, metaphors, and subjects, and as the location of and occasion for poetic meditations. Such attention was in some sense predicted by a few earlier poems, "Winter Sunrise," "Winter Fear," and "Stumps," but in most of Davison's previous work his use of natural fact was abstract and, as it were, incidental. In the new poems of *Walking the Boundaries*, however, concrete description of a natural world that retains its identity while rising into metaphor is often essential. This is true of a number of poems, "At the Close," "Lovers by Sea-Light," "Ground," and "Standing Fast: Fox into Hedgehog"—and of "Call Sign Aquarius," in which the speaker, pent up in a plastered room, is "deranged" but not out of range of the call of healing nature. However, this new quality is most obvious and most impressive in the four-part title sequence. Subtitled, respectively, "West by the Road," "South by the Wall," "East by the Cliff," and "North by the Creek," the quartet describes the boundary lines of Davison's Gloucester farm and events occurring within them—arranged not only by the cardinal directions indicated but also by the four seasons, fall and summer, winter and spring. In one sense, they are largely descriptive and less in need of comment than of exposure of their precise depictions, their matchings of mood to time and place. Here is a scene in late fall:

> The screech of a bluejay batters
> naked oak trunks, scattering
> bleached goldfinches
> wherever they cluster on thistles.
> The junco's tail flashes
> in the cedar. He sings
> of two pebbles chipping against one another.
>
> (65)

Here is one near the end of winter:

My breath is glue in my nostrils.
Mere air holds the sleeping marsh
solidly in chains, it crumples
the recent thaw's ruts
into hogback ridges
that the sun when it waxes
will take much trouble
to melt down again
into March mud.

(83)

However, the poems are more than such exposure would suggest. They also give rise to richly metaphoric meaning. This meaning is gradually produced by repeated descriptions of nature's un-self-conscious ability to at once resist, defend against, accept, and therefore in some sense survive the changes of time which bind it, which it somehow understands as both destructive and creative, the very limits and possibilities of life and self. A single example will do:

The thatch of the marsh holds hard:
it crouches down on matted fibers
to quake at air but yield its seed to water.
Come January, grumbling glaciers
will walk uphill in the arms
of northeast gales to shear
a year's marsh hay.

(65)

The spartina's combination of rigid resistance and yielding acceptance ensures both the clearing of ground for new seed and the survival of that seed, a perfect response to things as they are. Much is lost in the process: the same ice that will shear the marsh's hay will "macerate against the granite / piers of the bridge / the buried shells of snails," but life goes on; it learns to fit what is. Animals sense the winter's coming but wait without despair: "Their lungs / bloom like flowers / at the alienation of the air." Of course, such acceptance is easier for the instinctive, unthinking natural world than it is for self-conscious man, and in the first two poems of "Walking the Boundaries" the speaker is little more than a recording presence. This, too, begins to change in the third poem where it is now the rag end of winter and the speaker waits, on edge, like the rest of nature, for the coming spring. Like "woodpiles and slumbering straw," he nurses in his own way his own "reliquaries of calories / against the scorch of wind and the hiss of snow"; like the world, he sings his own lullaby "across the chasm / between this dangerous land / and the whispering sun." However, although the poet's very acts of walking his boundaries and acceding to their facts have been acts of fitting himself to his place, it remains rare for him or any man to cross the boundaries between self and nature into such unifying moments, and the final poem of the sequence, and the book, begins in separation:

> Inside my human walls I sit surrounded
> by scurrying music. Voices sing *Kyrie*.
> My eyesight ranges out across the field.
> Those acres tolerate us as their maker does,
> suffering denials without a sound,
> courtesies and rain without a smile.
>
> (91)

This is nature's indifference against the anguished yearning of the music of man's Mass, with its "unimaginable plea / that a Lamb should grant us peace." Yet there is connection as well; there is in nature, if not salvation, a yearning beyond limits, too. It is early spring, at evening. The poet leaves the house and witnesses the nuptial flight and song of the woodcock, that usually most earthbound and silent of local birds. His description is masterful in its detail and in its extension of detail to larger meaning:

As he leaves the earth his song ascends
higher and higher, pitch upon pitch, spiral
after spiral. At last, at the top of his helix
three hundred feet or more, it is enough,
he can rise no farther on the updraft of this song,
he has reached a boundary. He starts to fall.
He topples from the peak, repulsed by sky.
He dips zigzag then loops and twitters earthward,
his song hot on the wingbeats of his flight
coiling in chirrups of retreating tailspin.
Plunge and flutter. Silence. He glides
from the edge of light across the edge of dark
to alight upon the very shadowed patch
of earth from which the night had lifted him.
A pause for breath. He trumpets out a warning
that this was *not* a failure. He collects
himself to ascend again, to reach beyond
the edge of the habitable world, beyond
his limits of heaviness and incarnation.

(92)

The metaphors of constant struggle, of quest, of possibility and limit, of self and world, of spirit and flesh, of failure and success now grounded in and grown from fact, the poem can apply them to man and man's condition (bound and aching to be unbounded) to produce in wondrous music an affirmation wholly contained by fully accepted limits yet ever straining beyond them:

Body at least is bound within a landscape,
an earth that holds us fastened to the seasons
for food and footing, birth and burial.
Regardless of the gifts we've left behind
and all the boundaries we cannot cross,
some power lets us press beyond our powers:
echoes of wind, of ebb and flow, of heartbeat,
singing that trickles landward with the waters,
music that clambers skyward through the dark.

(93)

In this superb poem, its four parts enclosing and commenting on all the poems of *Walking the Boundaries*, in its natural voice, its brilliant merging of idea and fact, its central paradox of acceptance without complacence, Davison achieves the culmination of his poetry so far.

A Voice in the Mountain

Coming after the breakthroughs of *Walking the Boundaries*, Davisons's fifth book, *A Voice in the Mountain*, 1977, is. in some ways a disappointment, for it contains many poems that are badly flawed. In other and more important ways, however, it is also cause for celebration, for it has more excellent poems than any previous collection. Thematically, the new poems are consistent with those of earlier books. They are still focused by the search for knowledge of self and of how to live, although—again—with more acceptance and balance and less desperation than before. Elegies, poems on the family and other relations, an occasional statement of poetics, and many poems of indirect and direct social comment and criticism persist. On the other hand, poems directly concerned with psychological states are rare here. The major development in *A Voice in the Mountain*, however, is an intensification of one begun in *Walking the Boundaries* and the continuing result of Davison's achieved powers of acceptance and qualified affirmation: the shifting of the locus of the search for knowledge of the self and of how to live from the psychological to the natural and rural world, the shifting of his major source of language, image, and metaphor from psychology to landscape. There is also a slight and related shift toward a search for general meanings beyond the self and the world. This is not an about-face or inversion, for Davison remains a poet of great range and continues to draw materials and inspiration from a wide variety of places and experiences, but there is no doubt that the area from and in which his best and most characteristic poems are produced has changed.

In terms of technique, *A Voice in the Mountain* is more or less continuous with previous work. The speaker's voice is not so much more controlled as more in control. There is a return to more imposed forms (several quatrains, a sestina) and a little more rhyme than was typical in *Walking the Boundaries'* new poems, but Davison's characteristic mode seems now, as before, blank-verse and free-verse poems, often in structure-indicating stanzas. Occasional literary and other allusiveness, carefully managed ambivalence, and the use of irony—at its worst, too obvious irony—persists, as does the use of plain but reverberant diction.

Like Davison's first three books, *A Voice in the Mountain* is divided into, in this case, four titled sections. Because the first of these contains the preponderance, although not all, of the best of the book's thirty-one poems, and because it has the largest number of the nature poems that are most important to the book and to Davison's development, comment on it is reserved until last. The second section of *A Voice in the Mountain,* "The Dolls' House," has six poems, the two best of which, "The Fall of the Dolls' House" and "La Cathedrale Engloutie," like earlier poems, expose the destructive falseness of forced perfections which, in the language of "Peripheral Vision," "tidy up the view / And clear it out of true." Describing a town where the cathedral has been left intact outside and swallowed up inside, converted part to bank and part to banquet hall, the latter poem effectively exposes a classic contemporary ill, the bland or hedonistic materialism that remains when capitalism is cut off from its religious and ascetic roots.

Section three of *A Voice in the Mountain,* "The Hanging Man," has fewer good and more failed poems than the second. The title poem, for instance, falls prey to its own cleverness. However, two of the poems in this section are much better than the others. "Lamia" effectively suggests both the title myth of a female monster living on the flesh of youth and the ambivalent judgment of Keats's long poem of the same name in its own ambivalent portrait of a contemporary woman desperately afraid of illness, aging, and physical rejection. The best poem of this largely public group, though, is "The Compound Eye," an elegy for one of Davison's contemporaries, the poet L. E. Sissman, who died, as for ten years he had known he would, of Hodgkin's disease in 1976, and whose posthumous collected poems Davison edited and prefaced. It pays handsome tribute to Sissman's personal courage and to the compound seeing of his ordering art, and concludes with an assertion of Davison's preference for the imperfect disarray of life over any dainty perfection, an assertion tonally apt both in its clear judgment of Sissman's powers and limits and in the sense of loss it conveys: "From the postwar city / look out at the city of God, and then confess / how sweet was the disorder in the dress." (Compare Robert Herrick's "Delight in Disorder.")

The fourth section of *A Voice in the Mountain*, "Head Stone," is much better than the second and third; the title poem of the section is especially good. In his autobiography and in "Dark Houses" Davison mentions his scattering, at his father's wish, the father's ashes from a cliff facing a salt marsh on the son's Gloucester farm. "Head Stone" returns to that act, the cliff the monumental stone of the title, the poem the son's own headstone for his father. Indifferent to human time, to human presence or absence, the "great rock blazes high above the marsh"; it "glows / like old love letters," ripe with permanence and loss. The conclusion's exploration of the memorializing powers of matter and of mind is profoundly ambivalent: "It endures, no matter, / when no more dreams are stirring on the farm / and no true feeling leaves no memory." The stone endures both as matter, beyond human measurements, which do not matter, and as idea, its merely physical self "no matter." The last line plays once more on the ambiguities of Stendhal's apothegm. It suggests that the stone's memorial will prevail even when man is out of this world and in some other where true feeling does leave memory. It also suggests—"no true feeling leaves no memory" taken now as assertion— that the memory of the beloved dead will always remain in the minds of men. The combination of meaningful loss with meaningful confidence in continuities surpassing the self is finely elegiac.

"Head Stone's" skillfully managed ambivalence and its natural metaphors for human concerns make it an appropriate transition to the largest and best section of *A Voice in the Mountain*, its first, "Making Much of Orioles." Aside from the slightness of the rustically urbane "Lying in the Shade," which states the desire to "tell / a little of the way things are," aside from the minor ironies of "Circolo della Caccia" (the circle of hunters or hunt club) and the rather blunt statements on the predatory nature of predictive thought in "The Hawk of the Mind," these are among Davison's finest poems and on what seems more and more his poetry's main line. Several of them begin in natural description which gradually rises toward emblematic metaphor. "Zenith: Walker Creek" presents a series of finely heard and seen images for the slow high summer that follows and slackens the impassioned urgencies of spring ("The pheasant's declaration rings out half as often"; "the bay blooms with looser and larger sails"), but from their observation comes a surprising, then apt assertion of hoped-for fulfillments unfulfilled: "Those long days were the promises we broke." The dull circularities of human energies spent and lost arise to overwhelm as the natural year tips again toward fall. A related atmosphere of loss informs the enlargingly titled "Bicentennial." The flowers and birds its irregularly rhyming quatrains progressively describe carry the year from spring, through summer, toward fall. It ends with that image of woods invading fields, so crucial a metaphor for threat in the poetry of Frost, to suggest both a particular sense of loss and constriction in the ownership of a once-working farm now much reduced, and a more general sense of the unprogressively cyclic nature of national and human existence:

> Cattle might be lowing
>
> were trees not making motions
> to wipe our fields away.
> Two hundred years of farming?
> A single stand of hay.

(6)

An even darker loss is depicted in "Day of Wrath," where precisely rendered descriptions of the slowed down, dying world of a day in early fall ("September silence sags over the field"; "The marsh tides move like syrup") lead to a potent image of endless desolation:

> This afternoon is tangled in its silence
> until a yellow dog, posted to guard an empty house,
> lets out a howl. His desertedness will never end.
> No man will cross the road for his relief.
> His work of watching will go on forever.
>
> (9)

Not all the nature poems of *A Voice in the Mountain* are so unremittingly bleak. For instance, Davison's birthday poem for the then eighty-year-old author and friend of the poet and his father, J. B. Priestley, "Autumn Zodiac," employs the language of seasons, of planting and harvest, to suggest both the threat of time and change ("the cold caustic of our century / has scarred the promises that we believed") and time's continuing, cyclical promise ("Yet Virgo smiles at us like every wife / who owes her harvest to unclouded spring"). Complex treatments of natural imagery and setting appear in several other poems here as well, most of them involving metaphorical narrations of the author's experiences with the natural world.

"Making Much of Orioles" recalls the poet's attempt to rescue the brood of a pair of orioles that had nested in an elm tree on his land. After their chicks were hatched, but before they were fledged, the tree succumbed to Dutch elm disease, and the nest was left exposed. Hoping to save the young from being abandoned, he "pruned the dangling branch that held the nest / at its tip, like moss wrapped around a finger," and then tied it as high up in a chokecherry tree as he could reach. Surprisingly, and after an anxious wait, the parent birds responded to familiar cries from an unfamiliar site. The young were fed, fledged, and finally flew away. The speaker hung the "withered nest," "a trophy / of something like a victory of will," on his wall, "perhaps to hatch its meaning." "But a nest is no place to arrest a song / that in its very nature has no end"; by the second year the orioles, perhaps "his" nestlings, have built elsewhere. The nest is thrown "behind a lilac bush." The story is well told in precise language, but the poem's real interest arises from the way the story, in increasingly suggestive language ("something like a victory of will," "hatch its meaning," "arrest a song," "my nestlings," "I don't know"), gradually and naturally builds to a metaphor for the ambivalent connections and disconnections of man from nature, for the successes and failures in every act of man's effort to know, possess, and control his ultimately indifferent world.

"Cross Cut" employs a similar method. Davison narrates the felling of an old and dying pear tree to produce metaphors of both the junctures and disjunctions of human and natural time ("in age not quite / a century, perhaps, but twice as old as I am"; "You thrust erect as stiff as the memory of my oldest neighbor") and of the gains and losses of human intervention in the natural world (the tree was dangerous; it could have stood "for years, / heart eaten out, just fingering its life"; on the other hand, "Perhaps I could have helped you out of the air / with some shreds of your stature left intact, / but now I've failed you"; "Only inches above the nourishing ground /a cross-cut stump, stark white, reveals at bottom / you're still as lively as the day you bloomed").

"Skiing by Moonlight" recounts the act of its title, cross-country skiing on the poet's moonlit farm, and closes with an image of wild nature's invasion by night of the world the daylight lets us think we own:

> Our sheep have all taken shelter
> within the black barn.
> In the windless moonlight
> only an owl hoots against the cold
>
> while deer, silent among pines,
> wait to hear my skis stop hissing
> and the back door click shut

before they wade toward the rick
to steal some hay.

(13)

Again the themes, here those of imagined domesticity and posses-
sion, arise naturally from narrative and descriptive facts.
The themes that connect these poems also focus the more
public poetry of "Haskell's Mill," a narrative meditation on the
history of a now-decayed eighteenth-century mill that once ground
grain with the power generated from the controlled overflow of
a tidal creek. Like "House Holding" and "Insularity," this poem
too is sometimes overcome by the prose weight of versified his-
tory—a problem with the looser narrative mode Davison has
increasingly turned to and one he solves more satisfactorily in
shorter poems. Moreover, "Haskell's Mill" is sometimes overwritten
and sentimental ("Enlarging peasant patience with the craft / of
millers, moving stones by water, / men turned mere fodder into
manly meal"; "the shingled house of food"), and its contrasts can
seem simplistic in setting modern and urban evils ("The city
grows, a cancer between rivers") against older and rural perfec-
tions ("they planted corn and ground it into meal / without the
use of any other force / than nature's, than the mind's"). How-
ever, it is precisely its refusal of such simplifications that partially
saves the poem from these real faults. Finally, it is not time or
place that determines value here, but the wills and acts of men.
Haskell deserves tribute because "He kept the balance between
life and death, / the sun and moon, the water and the stone,"
but the speaker also recognizes that he was both "prostitute and
priest," his ritual as commercial as any in a modern city ("mind's"
in the quotation above also makes the point). Modern men deserve
criticism for their failures to unite themselves with the fundamental
facts of nature, but the fault is clearly in them and not in any
where or when:

Our farms are farmland only in the deed
and finally revert to wilderness
because no one of us has got the heart
to keep his hopes alive.

(15)

Perhaps the poem's flaws are fatal, but its clear-eyed, inclusive ambivalence, its sometimes effective language (for instance, the intricacies suggested by "in the deed" in the passage above), and the largeness of scope that suggests a merging of public with more private themes all promise better things to come. The same might be said of this entire volume, which—largely because it is working away from an old and toward a new and different focus—has nearly as many failed as first-rate poems: its best poems and even some of its worst promise better things to come. The final poem of *A Voice in the Mountain*'s first section is "Thanksgiving." Its affirming acceptance of the ambiguities of gifts (in Swedish, the word means "marriage," in German, "poison") extends the fine earlier poem "Gifts" and points to what will be a major concern of Davison's next, most recent, and best book. Its skillfully handled natural metaphor looks back to the breakthroughs of his last two books and forward to those of the next one.

Barn Fever and Other Poems

Barn Fever (1981) is Davison's best book, best because in it his familiar themes are treated with increased and consistent technical skill and tonal control, and because, more fully and clearly than before, its poems explore and meditate on the self and its relations to others and the world, while remaining centered in a developing vision of the complexly double nature of man and the place he inhabits. Thematically, then, *Barn Fever* is continuous with Davison's prior work. It is technically continuous as well. There are a few poems in conventional forms, rhymed and unrhymed quatrains, a villanelle, and a few in symmetrical stanzas, but most of these poems are in tight or loose iambics, in versions of blank verse, or in free verse (although even in these there often remains a roughly iambic base). The diction continues to be marked by fertile plainness. Ambiguity and allusiveness, especially biblical allusiveness, persist. The merging of explorations of self and natural world that began in *Walking the Boundaries* and intensified in *A Voice in the Mountain* is continued here in many poems in which enlarging metaphors arise from descriptive and narrative fact.

The twenty-five new poems of *Barn Fever* (there is also a fine dedicatory poem to the author's wife, a tribute to her writing and to her gifts to his) are divided, more or less by subject matter, into four sections. The first, "Pastures and Meadows," has six poems that describe and narrate scenes and events on Davison's farm. They are directly in the line of poems like "Walking the Boundaries," "Zenith: Walker Creek," "Skiing by Moonlight," "Cross Cut," and "Haskell's Mill." Like each of *Barn Fever*'s other sections, "Pastures and Meadows" has an epigraph drawing on one of the many and mixed meanings of the word *gift*. Here, the definition is: "With respect to real estate, formerly, any form of alienation." The suggestions in it of possession and its loss, and of oneness with and separation from the land are most appropriate to what is to follow. Several of these poems are concerned with livestock. In symmetrical stanzas, "The Ram Beneath the Barn" describes in detail a sheep too wild for human contact:

> The droppings of a winter foul his straw,
> but I dare no longer venture to his level
> with grain, hay, water. I lower them to him
> as to a tribe closed off by mountain snows.
>
> (3)

Alienation seems complete, yet, as "venture to his level" begins perhaps to say, speaker and ram have something in common, anger, perhaps, resentment for containment, or for sexual satisfactions delayed. At any rate, after describing the servicing of ewes the ram will perform in fall, the poem ends with this conjunction:

"but in this March we stare each other down, / two rams caught in a thicket by the horns." In this last line implications of shared entrapment and lust are joined by those of Abraham's reward of a replacement for the sacrifice of Isaac to imply shared suffering in the name of some larger, mysterious, and necessary fate. Here, as elsewhere in these poems, contemplation of natural facts, of man's union and disunion with his world, gives rise to teasing thought.

"Lambkill" takes its title from a common name for sheep laurel, a field plant poisonous to livestock. It tells the story of the death from it of one of a flock of sheep let into a meadow to browse it into pasture. The poem has wonderfully precise evocations of such matters as plant succession and animal husbandry, pays tribute to the resisting and accepting courage of animals, and wonders about the implications of man's use of them to shape the world to his own needs. More important, however, the narrative is a subtle metaphor for human action and thought, for the possibilities, dangers, and limits of knowing and making. With that in mind, listen to this description of the reaction of the sheep to being moved from their simple pasture into the complex overgrowth of meadow:

> Waking, they browsed their way through the inscrutable,
> bawling out their wish for a view of level grass,
> hungry for simplicity. They thrust heads
> through the wiring of their fence to nibble lawn
> that stretched out ahead like understanding
> while cryptic stands of fodder rustled behind.
>
> (6)

Eventually, the sheep accomplish their job, their world is again made pasture, again makes sense, but mysteries are left behind in "cryptic stands" and the swallowed costs of poisonous complexities. There are limits to knowledge and life that no expansion of thought can cure. The veterinary doctoring doesn't take. A young ram dies. So do we all. Whether we advance civilization or merely simplify, that is our knowing's final limit, for we are all (as the nicely worked-in quotation from Yeats's "Sailing to Byzantium" has it) " 'fastened to a dying animal,' " and, as Yeats went on to say, we know not what we are. Not only does "Lambkill" deliver all this from rather ordinary fact, but it does so without seeming forced, without the prose flatness or false heightening that flawed efforts to get at such significance in some of the narrative meditations of *A Voice in the Mountain*.

Unlike these largely narrative poems, "Interval" is descriptive. It depicts that moment when the world expands and contracts to react to summer's end and the coming onset of winter. However, this is slight compared to the volume's long (136-line) title poem. Without the flatness and overwriting that mar such related earlier efforts as "Haskell's Mill" and "House Holding," "Barn Fever" retells the natural and human history of the two-hundred-year-old barn on Davison's Gloucester property. Gradually, its detailed narration of this particular barn's decline becomes a representative history of our own long decline from connection with the land. The owners grow more and more eccentric: old maids; a Harvard anthropologist who tames the grass to lawn, then sells because the country has become too tame; a State Street lawyer afraid that Boston will be bombed. The farm shrinks; the barn loses its central place; the house takes over and is "infected by the suburbs"; the barn is left to be vandalized and to rot. The social criticism thus implied is largely left to speak for itself, and the poem usually avoids the sometimes sentimental indignation of earlier versions of its theme. What really gives it weight, however, is its conclusion. When Davison bought the farm, he partly healed the barn and put the livestock back on the land, but he is at best a part-time farmer. He recognizes that, recognizes also that the very act of writing this poem is part of the long history of abstraction that doomed the barn, that removes us all from the fundamental facts and processes of life:

> Without the barn there would be little cause
> to call this piece of land more than a piece
> of land, one corner of it fastened down
> by a yellow house where people sit and write
> about the days when the farm had farmers on it
> as well as the busiest barn for miles around.
>
> (11-12)

Sentiment ("Malachi and Mary Brown did more than play. / They metamorphosed grass into milk and butter, / kernels and clamshells into hens and eggs") and nostalgia for a lost way of life are in these lines, but there is neither escapism nor sentimentality in the poet's understanding of the boundaries of his self and place. In poems like this, attention to place becomes a mode of knowledge.

The second section of *Barn Fever* is called "The Sound of Wings." It again has a definition of "gift" an epigraph: "Some quality or endowment given to man by God or a deity," and the entire section insists on the doubleness of everything, insists that even moments of seeming transcendence occur within and not outside the always qualifying complexities of life. The opening poems are descriptions of present moments, bird song at dawn, the seeding of marsh grass, but if these are moments of refuge, they offer no escape from time or meaning. "Thatch," for instance, describes a surrender of self to future. "July Meeting" is timebound and raises matters of precedence, pattern, and order. The remaining poems of "The Sound of Wings" insist more clearly still that there is no escape from the complexities of the past, of self, of time, of thought, that whatever blessedness there is occurs only within their confines, in their context.

This is the burden of one of Davison's finest poems, "Paradise as a Garden," based on the myths of Eden and the fall. The opening stanza defines a paradox in which limitation and freedom, contentment and desire, death and life, and timelessness and time are joined. Its image is a garden "in which what enlarges the space / is its surrounding hedges," in which "husk and flower are one." This is paradise. But any unbalancing to either pole empties it of itself. If the container is removed to emphasize its content, then only sprawl is left. If boundaries are all there are, "bracelets of stone and water," then the garden loses leaf and fruit and flower. Blessedness for Davison is not exclusion, then, but inclusion, context. Nothing is, except with something else:

> And so it follows, through ages, crosses and tongues,
> that when we speak of our eternal delight,
> whether a garden we were once expelled from
> or one that has been lost and overgrown,
> it is the edges we cannot forget.
> Whatever persists within, forever fresh,
> is the indelible border of imagination.
>
> (21)

This is man's condition: he constantly falls from the paradise where the opposites that make him what he is can be contained in balance; he constantly imagines his return.

The section's title poem is also concerned with paradox and also takes its images from the natural world. "The Sound of Wings" describes the coming on of winter and insists on the paradox of changeless change, the oneness of the natural cycle's parts, and the presence of continuity and loss, of present, past, and future in any given moment. It makes and even enacts its point by breaking its sequence into sections nonetheless united, each labeled with one of the four elements once thought to make the world, each modified by one of a pair of opposites the scene contains: "Perfect Fire" and "Imperfect Water," "Future Earth" and "Present Air." An experience of vision within the context of such defining limits is the subject of "Elsewhere in Colorado," in which the speaker, alien in the alienating world of business, advertising presentations, and nameless dinner parties, is suddenly vouchsafed a glimpse of "an oriole blazing orange" on high.

The insistence on context described here is, of course, another version of the demand for inclusion that has always focused

Davison's art. Always essential to such inclusion has been recognition of the antecedents of personal past. The four-part sequence "Atmospheres" involves that past, and other contexts as well. Its free verse poems record four autobiographical experiences in Colorado. The first, "*Boulder 1935*," is from Davison's boyhood. Using facts and metaphors drawn from Boulder's peculiarities of atmospheric pressure, the poem recalls childhood environments both protective and threatening: "day . . . seldom darkened / except with stormclouds or dust / that blew west from the poisoned plains." In "*Cheyenne Mountain 1944*" the speaker recollects a mountain-climbing adventure with a group of schoolmates, all of them sixteen. Its inclusion is of the mix of memory and loss. The poem records a Wordsworthian moment of timelessness in the sighting of a bighorn sheep: "Motion and sound both ceased." Timeful as well as timeless, the moment ends when one of the boys charges the ram with his geologist's pick. It easily escapes. So far, the poem has changelessly contained both the changelessness and the change of the remembered experience. Then, aware that as the present is only understood through the past so the past is only understood through the present, it proceeds, as it did with the timeless encounter with the ram, to replace its larger memory in time: "Now decades later, Gifford is dead, / and only a cramped gathering of bighorns / camps, above timberline."

The third poem of the sequence, "*National Center for Atmospheric Research 1967*," records an adult visit to that institution. Here context is present, as it were, by its absence, for the Center's scientists are disconnected from the whole of life: the windows of the building are tinted "just enough to admit / all elements of the light except glare, / brilliance without dazzle." The scientists' abstraction permits them intellectual concern with the geometric growth of population, but closes them off from other facts and feelings, here the snow-eating wind of spring:

> Their house
> of inquiry shelters without surprise
> the earth's commotion, while
> the chinook breathes warmly
> on dissolving snow.
>
> (28–29)

The last poem of the "Atmospheres" sequence, "*Boulder 1979*," returns to the present, describes the poet's working with a potter, and uses the metaphors of firing, glazing, and cooling clay to describe the need for man to accept the paradox of made and making life, of death and life, and of his place in constant, constantly changing natural cycles:

> We carry our unfired flesh
> through atmospheres and climates
> that wait for our decay,
> expecting things alive
> to take on the life of things.
> Change drifts down on our heads
> from a past mediated
> by mason, shaman, priest—
> all those who learned the secret
> that the seed must be buried to live,
> caught up in atmospheres,
> loosening into vapor,
> tightening into snowflake.
>
> (30)

The last poem of "The Sound of Wings" is "Il Se Sauve"; the title is idiomatic French for "he saves himself" or "he escapes." Its suggestions of salvation and escapism are both pertinent, for the poem (a gloss on John Cheever's prison novel, *Falconer*) is again concerned with the paradox of mankind's dual nature, his mix of flesh and spirit, animal and angel, and thus the mix of finally indistinguishable urges to salvation and escape in everything he does. A balanced sense of possibilities and limits again results:

> Among shadows and sentences you remember
> when you could have made a break for it,
> when, if you had had the wings of an angel,
> you could have got out of here,
> uplifted, saved yourself.
>
> (32)

As its title suggests, the third section of *Barn Fever*, "Men Working," turns from the relatively philosophical concerns of the first two sections to those more public and social ones that have always been an important if minor part of Davison's work. These poems of social commentary and social criticism are among the best he has written. However, two poems that are more obviously continuous with, transitional from, the poems of "The Sound of Wings" should be considered first. Containing commentary on Old Testament texts, as the title indicates, "Three Midrashim" insists on paradox and context. Its first two parts can be understood as prayers for enlargements of self, but its third, "Darkheart," most clearly exposes the poet's continuing concern with the human tensions of flesh and spirit, acceptance and desire, the boundaries within which blessedness is met. This the complex self resists as it recognizes:

> How graceless to deny
> that grunt of understanding:
> that only *in my flesh*
> *shall I see God!*
>
> (40)

From a quite different angle, "Life Work" exposes the danger implicit in such rejection of the unalterable limits of one's human condition. In it, in order to exemplify that danger, Davison uses the case of his father's lifelong and in ways debilitating shame at his (the father's) being born out of wedlock. Since such facts, like our mortality, the containment of our spirits in flesh, cannot be changed, "Since change has more to do / with life than even life," such shame is (as the "waste of shame" reference to Shakespeare's Sonnet 129 makes clear) an "expense of spirit," a falsifying effort to prevent the unpreventable that alienates the self from the self and the world.

As noted above, the more public poems here are among Davison's best of this sort, largely because they escape the sometimes earlier fault of shrillness and because humor and control keep them from self-righteousness. The sort of social comment and criticism they invoke is suggested by the epigraph for this section, again a definition of "gift": "Something given to corrupt. A bribe." "Short Weight" is representative. In it the story of the departure of the one-time fixture of the public scribe satirizes the takeover of language by advertisers and governments and their reduction of its use from the essential to the commercial, from communication to exploitation, from telling truth to selling lies.

Continuing the exploration of the qualifying double context in which we live, in which all we do takes place, the final section of *Barn Fever* is called "Mixed Blessings," for Davison, the only ones there are. Its epigraph indicates once more the ambivalent significance of gifts and employs meanings of the word in other languages to make its point. In German, "gift" can mean "Poison, toxin, virus, venom, virulence, malice, fury"; in Swedish it means "Marriage" (compare the earlier "Thanksgiving"). The doubleness of pleasure and pain, joy and sorrow, ecstasy and anguish that informs the relationships of lovers, of husbands and wives, is the subject of these poems. The very terms "marriage" and "Poison" are the counters in the finely made villanelle "Sleeping Beauty Variations," which riddles the paradox of creative union and self-destructive self-sacrifice contained in the "gift" of love. In statement and symbolic landscape, "January 1977" defines the touching and destructive anguish felt by a lover at his loved one's physical absence. In "New Year's Eve" a disturbed dream of past lovers suggests love's (and memory's) ability both to intensify and to annihilate time. "On Ithaca" returns once again to *The Odyssey* (see "Travelling Among Islands," "Words for My Father," and "Calypso"), this time to explore the ambiguities of excitement and danger in public life and of boredom and security in domestic life. These are all good poems. However, the major work of this final section is the eight-part sequence about the poet's reaction to his wife's illness with cancer, "Wordless Winter."[16] Its opening poems, *"Clinical Depression"* and *"The Clinic"* describe the speaker's initial response, his slide from ordinary depression into the clinical state of anxiety (effectively expressed by the absence of ordering punctuation) and his distraught sense of responsibility and guilt for her disease. In the next two poems the speaker is more controlled. In *"Willing Her to Live"* he admits his wife is dying, but, he hopes, perhaps "no faster than anyone else." He is manuring his garden, and the fall earth is, as it were, excited by the prospects of spring. However, neither the defenses of gallows humor nor the promise of natural cycle avails here. The irrelevance of the individual in any wider scheme of things is overwhelming:

> Earth snatches compost back
> like a transfusion and will not pause
> to keep a leaf attached
> in response to prayers or tears
> or the use of shovels.
>
> (53)

The images of prayers and tears and shovels clearly convey the speaker's obsessive fear. In *"Frozen Drought"* the natural world reflects his own despair.

The obvious implication of the sequence's overall title, "Wordless Winter," is that one effect of his wife's illness on the poet is to leave him unable to write. His painful, self-protective withdrawal from poetry and his other interests and pursuits is recorded in *"Householder"*: "I have been taught by mixed blessings, / poisoned apples, / to sit apart, muscles clenched like marble." However understandable this is, however rooted in past experience of the mix of evil and good in all, it is nevertheless a refusal of the inclusion of context *Barn Fever* has everywhere called for and praised. The refusal is overcome in *"Stalemate,"* in which the speaker turns his attention from himself to his wife, accepts the poisoned apples of her courage and pain, and recognizes her successful containment of life's complexity:

> Her face, a landscape, carries
> the colors of contending forces:
> a tug of joy, eyes lit with laughter;
> a nagging hermit mask;
> a cloud of pain.
>
> (56)

The cancer is not defeated, but neither is its victim. For now at least there is a standoff. This does not produce release; the threat remains, as the images of persistent past and mysterious future and the puns on the word "arrested" in *"After Winter Slaughtering"* insist, and as does the more terrifying pun in *"Stalemate."* However, the speaker has found his words again; inspired by his wife's exemplary courage, he can face the complex facts and write. This too is not victory, but stalemate. As the metaphor of remembered penmanship training in the poem's last section, *"The Writing Lesson,"* shows, writing does not overcome but contains pain. No, not victory, but for living men in the real world where every blessing is mixed the only victory there can be. In writing, in including rather than fleeing complex facts, the mind and body are again in motion, beyond the "ebb-tide of emotion," beyond the "muscles clenched like marble," beyond the "Frozen Drought" of wordlessness.

Having earned this much relief, Davison concludes *Barn Fever* with "My Lady the Lake," a poem that is more abstract than those just discussed, but that still stresses the idea of the mixed blessing. Its lover is an image of self rather than another, but it, too, is centered by a vision of human paradox: "Still water gives us only a reflection. / Whatever we cast in, it will accept, / and in such lakes within the lake we drown." The self we see and make in our acts of self-reflection is what destroys us; this is our fate. Still, in our reflection we create and choose that self; this is responsibility, our freedom. This is who and what we are, our ambivalent gift, the poisoned marriage and mixed blessing of ourselves.

A Final Word

Peter Davison's real connection with New England both as place and as literary tradition is in the nature poetry that more and more dominates his recent work. In that poetry, a specifically New England rural landscape typically provides the details, images, metaphors, and locations for his exploration of self and world. In it, a post-transcendentalist, Frostian mode where natural detail and event both are and are not seen as emblematic of human meaning is increasingly the characteristic method of those explorations. This connection could be pushed too far; Davison remains a poet of great range, of many subjects and modes, but there is no doubt that in the senses described New England now focuses his work.

As Davison's relationships with New England require qualification, so do descriptions of his place within the movements of contemporary poetry. In its adherence to formal conventions, its concern with craft, its all-inclusiveness, its use of irony, and its almost constant ambivalence, Davison's work is surely tied to traditional poetry and to the orthodoxies of the academic mode. However, in its relatively accessible meanings (his poetry is almost never wilfully difficult, and rarely metaphysical in the literary sense), in its essentially if somewhat distanced autobiographical nature (recalling that the shift from impersonal to personal may well be the most fundamental of contemporary developments), in its formal loosening, and in its frequent attention to dream states and states of psychological extremity, his work is just as surely tied to contemporary rejections and replacements of those traditions and orthodoxies. Still, a modernist rather than post-modernist sense of man's and the world's fundamental, ironic, and tragic doubleness always informs that work. Qualifications could continue.

Perhaps it is best simply to say again with Daniel Hoffman that his poems "are both formal and contemporary in feeling." More important than any of this is that Davison has written and continues to write, with increasing imagination and skill, a poetry of great and moral attention to the multiple boundaries of self, family, society, and natural world, a poetry in which a constant effort is made to clarify the self, the world, and life, not so much to make them clear, as to see clearly what they are, to recognize and accept their unchangeable limits, and to make the most of their available possibilities. In walking his boundaries, in enlarging them to include the human as well as personal self, he has given us again and again, in that phrase of Frost he has quoted himself, "a figure of the will braving alien entanglements."

Notes and References

Chapter One

1. For a straightforward survey of these groups, their members, and their technical and thematic attitudes, see Karl Malkoff, *Crowell's Handbook of Contemporary American Poetry* (New York: Thomas Y. Crowell, 1973).

Chapter Two

1. William Meredith, quoted in John Wakeman, ed., *World Authors, 1950–1970: A Companion Volume to Twentieth Century Authors* (New York: H. W. Wilson, 1975), p. 977. (Throughout the biographical sketch I am indebted to this work for information and to the Meredith entries in James Vinson and D. L. Kirkpatrick, eds., *Contemporary Poets*, 2d ed. (New York: St. Martin's, 1975), pp. 1035–36; Clare D. Kinsman and Mary Ann Tennenhouse, eds., *Contemporory Authors: A Bio-Bibliographical Guide to Current Authors and Their Works*, 1st rev. (Detroit: Gale Research Co., 1974), 9–12, 619; and the 1978–79 edition of *Who's Who in America*.)

2. Quoted in Wakeman, *World Authors*, p. 978.

3. Quoted in Gregory FitzGerald and Paul Ferguson, "The Frost Tradition: A Conversation with William Meredith," *Southwest Review* 57 (1972):115.

4. Richard Howard, "William Meredith: 'All of a Piece and Clever and at Some Level, True,' " in *Alone with America: Essays on the Art of Poetry in the United States Since 1950* (New York: Atheneum, 1971), p. 319.

5. William Meredith, *Love Letter from an Impossible Land* (New Haven, 1944; rpt. New York, 1971), p. 32. Unless otherwise noted,

189

the poems quoted in each section of this chapter are from the volume under discussion. The longer quotations separated from the text are referenced by page numbers in parentheses.

6. Quoted in Wakeman, *World Authors*, p. 978.

7. Quoted in FitzGerald and Ferguson, "The Frost Tradition," p. 110.

8. Henry Taylor, " 'In Charge of Morale in a Morbid Time.' The Poetry of William Meredith," *Hollins Critic* 16 (1979):3.

9. Thomas Landless, "New Urns for Old: A Look at Six Recent Volumes of Verse," *Sewanee Review* 81 (1973):148.

10. Dudley Fitts, "Meredith's Second Volume," *Poetry* 73 (1948): 111.

11. This is said despite Meredith's attractive and partially convincing defense of the practice in *Ships and Other Figures, The Open Sea*, and elsewhere.

12. William Meredith, "The Luck of It," in *American Poets in 1976*, ed. William Heyen (Indianapolis, Ind.: Bobbs-Merrill, 1976), p. 193.

13. See Meredith's own comment on this matter in FitzGerald and Ferguson, "The Frost Tradition," p. 109.

14. Howard, in *Alone With America*, p. 324.

15. Quoted in FitzGerald and Ferguson, pp. 115 and 114.

16. William Meredith, "In Loving Memory of the Late Author of *The Dream Songs*," in *John Berryman: A Checklist*, ed. Richard J. Kelley (Metuchen, N.J.: The Scarecrow Press, 1972), p. xix.

17. Ibid., p. xv.

18. Quoted in FitzGerald and Ferguson, "The Frost Tradition," pp. 111–12.

19. The quotation is from Percy Bysshe Shelley, *Prometheus Unbound*, I, ll:192–99.

20. Peter Davison, "Madness in the New Poetry," *Atlantic*, January 1965, p. 93.

21. Dudley Fitts, "The Sweet Side of Right," *Saturday Review*, 22 March 1958, p. 23.

Chapter Three

1. All quotations in the first two paragraphs are from John Wakeman, ed., *World Authors, 1950–1970: A Companion Volume to Twentieth Century Authors* (New York: H. W. Wilson, 1975),

pp. 183–84. (Throughout the biographical sketch I am indebted to this work for information and to the Booth entries in James Vinson and D. L. Kirkpatrick, eds., *Contemporary Poets*, 2d ed. (New York: St. Martin's, 1975), pp. 148–49; Barbara Harte and Carolyn Riley, eds., *Contemporary Authors: A Bio-Bibliographical Guide to Current Authors and Their Works*, 1st rev. (Detroit: Gale Research Co., 1974):5–8, 127–28; and the 1978–79 edition of *Who's Who in America*.)

2. Philip Booth quoted in Richard Jackson, "Lives We Keep Wanting to Know: An Interview with Philip Booth," *Poetry Miscellany* 8 (1978):22.

3. Philip Booth, [Comments on the Poet's Voice], in *The Distinctive Voice*, ed. William J. Martz (Glenview, Ill.: Scott, Foresman, 1966), p. 252.

4. Philip Booth, *Letter from a Distant Land* (New York, 1957), p. 20. Unless otherwise noted, the poems quoted in each section of this chapter are from the volume under discussion. The longer quotations separated from the text are referenced by page numbers in parentheses.

5. I am indebted for this phrase to Professor Robert Cording of Holy Cross College.

6. John R. Wiggins, " 'To Live on a Cold Coast on the Edge of a Cold Sea,' " *Ellsworth American*, 8 November 1967, p. 9.

7. John Holmes, "Booth's New Poems," *Christian Science Monitor*, 4 January 1962, p. 11.

8. In line 14 of this poem, *Margins* misprints "now" for "how."

9. Booth, quoted in Jackson, "Lives," p. 22.

10. Ibid., p. 24.

11. Booth, "How a Poem Happens," in *50 Contemporary Poets: The Creative Process*, ed. Alberta A. Turner (New York: David McKay, 1977), p. 56.

12. Booth, quoted in Jackson, "Lives," p. 24.

13. Ibid., p. 25.

14. Booth comments on his sense of line in *Epoch* 29 (1980):173–75.

15. Booth has commented, in fine prose, on his relationship with Lowell during these years in "Summers in Castine, Contact Prints: 1955–1965," *Salmagundi* 37 (1977):37–53.

16. Booth, "Journey Out of a Dark Forest" [Review of Frost's *In the Clearing*], *New York Times Book Review*, 25 March 1962, p. 1.

Chapter Four

1. Davison tells his own story in intimate and penetrating detail in his autobiography, *Half Remembered* (New York, 1973).

2. Edwin Briggs, "Middle-Point Reflections," *Boston Globe*, 31 August 1973, p. 17.

3. Davison, *Half Remembered*, p. 186.

4. " 'Did Shriner Die or Make it to New York?': A Preface," in *Hello Darkness: The Collected Poems of L. E. Sissman*, ed. Peter Davison (Boston: Little Brown, Atlantic Monthly Press, 1978), p. x.

5. Daniel Hoffman, "Poetry: Dissidents from Schools," in *Harvard Guide to Contemporary American Writing*, ed. Daniel Hoffman (Cambridge: Harvard University Press, 1979), p. 579.

6. See Davison, *Half Remembered*, pp. 183–84, and Davison's "Time and the Poet," *The Writer*, August 1967, p. 20.

7. Davison, *Half Remembered*, pp. 184–86.

8. James Schevill, "Poets Ascend the Technical Trend," *Saturday Review*, 4 July 1964, p. 30.

9. Peter Davison, *The Breaking of the Day* (New Haven, 1964), p. 5. Unless otherwise noted, the poems quoted in each section of this chapter are from the volume under discussion. The longer quotations separated from the text are referenced by page numbers in parentheses.

10. See Dudley Fitts, "Foreword," in *The Breaking of the Day*, pp. vii–viii.

11. David Galler, "Three Recent Volumes," *Poetry* 110 (1967): 269.

12. Recounted in Davison, *Half Remembered*, pp. 169–72.

13. May Swenson, "Cheek by Jowl: Eight Poets," *Southern Review*, n.s. 7 (1971):958.

14. Archilochus, fragment 17, in *Greek Lyrics*, trans. Richard Lattimore (Chicago: University of Chicago Press, 1955), p. 3.

15. Isaiah Berlin, in *Russian Thinkers*, ed. Henry Hardy and Aileen Kelley (New York: The Viking Press, 1978), pp. 22–81.

16. Jane Davison died of cancer in the summer of 1981, a few months after the publication of *Barn Fever*, and after this study was completed.

Selected Bibliography

William Meredith

PRIMARY SOURCES

1. Books (Poetry)
The Cheer. New York: Knopf, 1980.
Earth Walk: New and Selected Poems. New York: Knopf, 1970.
Hazard, the Painter. New York: Knopf, 1975.
Love Letter from an Impossible Land. The Yale Series of Younger Poets. New Haven, Conn.: Yale University Press, 1944. Reprint edition: New York: AMS Press, 1971.
The Open Sea and Other Poems. New York: Knopf, 1958.
Ships and Other Figures. Princeton, N.J.: Princeton University Press, 1948.
The Wreck of the Thresher and Other Poems. New York: Knopf, 1958.

2. Translations
Alcools: Poems 1898–1913 by Guillaume Apollinaire. Garden City, N.Y.: Doubleday, 1964.

3. Articles
"The Frost Tradition: A Conversation with William Meredith" [Interview with Gregory FitzGerald and Paul Ferguson]. *Southwest Review* 57 (Spring 1972):108–17.
"In Loving Memory of the Late Author of *The Dream Songs*." In *John Berryman: A Checklist*, compiled by Richard J. Kelley. Metuchen, N.J.: Scarecrow Press, 1972.

"Introduction," with Mackie L. Jarrell. *Eighteenth Century Minor Poets*. Edited by Mackie L. Jarrell and William Meredith. New York: Dell, 1968.

"Introduction." *Shelley*. Edited by William Meredith. New York: Dell, 1962.

"The Language of Poetry in Defense of Human Speech: Some Notes on the Topic of the Struga Symposium of 1979." *American Poetry Review* 8 (November/December 1979):14–15.

"The Luck of It." *American Poets in 1976*. Edited by William Heyen. Indianapolis: Bobbs-Merrill, 1976.

SECONDARY SOURCES

Howard, Richard. "William Meredith: 'All of a Piece and Clever and at Some Level, True.'" *Alone With America: Essays on the Art of Poetry in the United States Since 1950*. New York: Atheneum, 1971, pp. [318]–26. Among the few essential pieces on Meredith so far. Examines the volumes from *Love Letter from an Impossible Land* through *The Wreck of the Thresher* with emphasis on Meredith's growth and on his testimony "to the war between delight and order" and "the necessity of divising them in each other."

Ludwig, Richard M. "The Muted Lyrics of William Meredith." *Princeton University Library Chronicle* 25 (Autumn 1963):73–85. The earliest important piece on Meredith; includes an analytical essay on his first three volumes and a detailed checklist of his publications.

Taylor, Henry. " 'In Charge of Morale in a Morbid Time': The Poetry of William Meredith." *Hollins Critic* 16 (February 1979):[1]–15. The most important study of Meredith so far, covering the poetry from *Love Letter from an Impossible Land* through *Hazard, the Painter*. Meredith continually finds "fresh ways of reminding us that there is joy in plucking at the hems of even the darkest mysteries."

Philip Booth

PRIMARY SOURCES

1. Books (Poetry)
Available Light. New York: Viking Press, 1973.
Before Sleep. New York: Viking Press, 1980.
The Islanders. New York: Viking Press, 1961.
Letter from a Distant Land. New York: Viking Press, 1957.
Margins: A Sequence of New and Selected Poems. New York: Viking Press, 1970.
Weathers and Edges. New York: Viking Press, 1966.

2. Articles
[Comments on the Poet's Voice]. In *The Distinctive Voice: Twentieth Century American Poetry.* Edited by William J. Martz. Glenview, Ill.: Scott Foresman, 1966, p. 252.
Headnote. *Maine Lines: 101 Contemporary Poems about Maine.* Compiled by Richard Aldridge. Philadelphia: J.B. Lippincott, 1970, p. 29.
"How a Poem Happens." *50 Contemporary Poets: The Creative Process.* Edited by Alberta A. Turner. New York: David McKay, 1977, p. 56.
"Image and Idea." *Literature for Adolescents.* Edited by Stephen Dunning and Alan B. Howes. Glenview, Ill.: Scott, Foresman, 1975, pp. 49–52.
"Lives We Keep Wanting to Know: An Interview with Philip Booth" [with Richard Jackson]. *Poetry Miscellany* 8 (1978):21–26.
[On the Poetic Line]. *Epoch* 29 (Winter 1980):173–75.
"Summers in Castine, Contact Prints: 1955–1965." *Salmagundi* 37 (Spring 1977):[37]–53.
"Thoughts on Language and Literature." *Vermont Academy Life,* Fall-Winter 1979–80, p. 14.

SECONDARY SOURCES

Stern, Milton R. "Halfway House: The Poems of Philip Booth."
  Twentieth Century Literature 4 (January 1959):148–53. The
  only extended piece on Booth's writing so far, and, although it
  discusses only his first book, by far the most serious and im-
  portant piece. Stern places Booth's work in the context of New
  England transcendentalism, insists that his themes "grow out of
  an ethical use of nature that becomes a re-exploration of the
  potentialities of American experience," and locates his work in a
  "halfway house" between a recognition of the world as a waste-
  land, "a commercialistic miasma," and a hope "for the sanative
  and rejuvenating possibilities of nature."

Wiggins, John R. " 'To Live on a Cold Coast On the Edge of a Cold
  Sea.' " *Ellsworth* [Maine] *American*, 8 November 1967, p. 9. A
  "profile" of Booth, exploring (with Booth's help) his ancestry,
  his life in Maine, his career, and his thoughts about life and
  literature. A useful introduction to the man.

Peter Davison

PRIMARY SOURCES

1. Books
   Poetry:
Barn Fever and Other Poems. New York: Atheneum, 1981.
The Breaking of the Day. The Yale Series of Younger Poets. New Haven, Conn.: Yale University Press, 1964.
The City and the Island. New York: Atheneum, 1966.
Dark Houses. Cambridge, Mass.: Halty Ferguson, 1971.
Pretending to Be Asleep. New York: Atheneum, 1970.
A Voice in the Mountain. New York: Atheneum, 1977.
Walking the Boundaries: Poems 1957–1974. New York: Atheneum, 1974.
   Autobiography:
Half Remembered: A Personal History. New York: Harper and Row, 1973.

2. Articles
" 'Did Shriner Die or Make It to New York?': A Preface," *Hello Darkness: The Collected Poems of L. E. Sissman.* Edited by Peter Davison. Boston: Little Brown; Atlantic Monthly Press, 1978, pp. vii–xiii.
"The Great Predicament of Poetry." *Atlantic*, June 1973, pp. 93–94, 96.
"Madness in the New Poetry." *Atlantic*, January 1965, pp. 90–93.
"New Poetry." *Atlantic*, July 1959, pp. 73–76; December 1963, pp. 82–85.
"New Sounds, New Silences." *Atlantic*, January 1971, pp. 96–98.
"Self-Revelation in the New Poetry." *Atlantic*, November 1961, pp. 170–79.
"Time and the Poet." *The Writer*, August 1967, pp. 20–21.
"To Live Life as a Poem . . . : An Interview with Peter Davison" [with Melissa Baumann]. *North Shore '75* [weekend magazine supplement of Essex Country Newspapers], 16 August 1975, pp. 1–3.

SECONDARY SOURCES

Parini, Jay. "In the Presence of What Is There: Wendell Berry and Peter Davison." *Virginia Quarterly Review* 54 (Autumn 1978): 762–68. Includes review of *A Voice in the Mountain*. Important for naming Davison "one of America's finest contemporary poets" and concentrating on his select use of personal experience, his diverse personae and unifying equipoise, his focus on natural symbols in poems in a Frostian bucolic mode, and his abundant humor.

Young, Vernon. "Raptures of Distress." *Parnassus: Poetry in Review* 3 (Spring/Summer 1975):75–89. Reviews *Walking the Boundaries*. Important for its attention to Davison's treatment of death and his "poetry of topographical change," and for its enthusiastic judgment of him as "one of the few poets of the first order writing English today."

Index